Ça Va ?

Mary Culpan

BELL & HYMAN

Also available:

Teachers' Booklet
(Tapescripts)   ISBN 0 7231 0882 X

Cassette Tape   0 7135 2822 2

Published by BELL & HYMAN
An imprint of Unwin Hyman Limited
Denmark House
37–39 Queen Elizabeth Street
London SE1 2QB

© Mary Culpan 1985

First published in 1985 by University Tutorial Press Limited
Reprinted by Bell & Hyman 1987

All rights reserved. No part of this publication may
be reproduced, stored in a retrieval system, or
transmitted in any form or by any means, electronic,
mechanical, photocopying, recording, or otherwise,
without the prior permission of Bell & Hyman.

ISBN 0 7135 2833 8

Typeset by Goodfellow and Egan, Cambridge
Printed in Great Britain at The Bath Press, Avon

CONTENTS

DOSSIER 1
A LA MAISON
Reading comprehensions	2
Listening comprehensions	5
Grammar exercises	7
Travail oral	7
Travail écrit	9
Vocabulary	10
Grammar summary:	11
– subject pronouns	11
– reflexive pronouns	11
– use of pronoun 'on'	11
– present tense	12
– imperative	15

DOSSIER 2
LA FAMILLE ET LES AMIS
Reading comprehensions	18
Listening comprehensions	24
Grammar exercises	25
Travail oral	26
Travail écrit	30
Vocabulary	33
Grammar summary:	34
– imperfect tense	34
– negatives	36
– 'qui' & 'que'	36

DOSSIER 3
AU COLLEGE
Reading comprehensions	38
Listening comprehensions	41
Grammar exercises	42
Travail oral	43
Travail écrit	44
Vocabulary	45
Grammar summary:	46
– asking questions	46
– comparisons	47

DOSSIER 4
ON FAIT DES COURSES
Reading comprehensions	50
Listening comprehensions	55
Grammar exercises	56
Travail oral	56
Travail écrit	58
Vocabulary	59
Grammar summary:	60
– 'du', 'de la', de l', 'des'	60
– direct object pronouns	60
– indirect object pronouns	61
– pronouns 'en' & 'y'	62

DOSSIER 5
SPORT ET LOISIRS
Reading comprehensions	64
Listening comprehensions	68
Grammar exercises	68
Travail oral	69
Travail écrit	71
Vocabulary	72
Grammar summary:	73
– perfect tense	73
– pluperfect tense	75
– emphatic pronouns	75
Revision test 1	76

DOSSIER 6
EN VACANCES
Reading comprehensions	80
Listening comprehensions	84
Grammar exercises	85
Travail oral	87
Travail écrit	88
Vocabulary	89
Grammar summary:	90
– future tense	90
– conditional tense	91
– après avoir + past participle	92
– prepositions with holiday & travel phrases	92

DOSSIER 7
AU TRAVAIL

Reading comprehensions	94
Listening comprehensions	96
Grammar exercises	97
Travail oral	97
Traval écrit	98
Vocabulary	100
Grammar summary:	100
– verbs followed by an infinitive	100
– verbs of communication	101
– translating 'in'	102
– translating 'for'	102

DOSSIER 8
ON ROULE!

Reading comprehensions	104
Listening comprehensions	107
Grammar exercises	107
Travail oral	109
Travail écrit	110
Vocabulary	112
Grammar summary:	113
– verb + 'à' + infinitive	113
– translating 'by'	113
– translating 'before'	114

DOSSIER 9
AU VOLEUR!

Reading comprehensions	116
Listening comprehensions	118
Grammar exercises	118
Travail oral	120
Travail écrit	121
Vocabulary	122
Grammar summary:	123
– verb + 'de' + infinitive	123
– translating 'about'	123
– more prepositions	124

DOSSIER 10
AU SECOURS!

Reading comprehensions	126
Listening comprehensions	129
Grammar exercises	130
Travail oral	130
Travail écrit	131
Vocabulary	131
Grammar summary:	132
– past historic tense	132
– changing direct to indirect speech	133
– more uses of the infinitive	134
Revision test 2	135

DOSSIER 11
REFERENCE SECTION

Numbers	140
Days, months, seasons	140
Dates	140
Times	141
Time expressions	141
Linking words and expressions	141
Other useful words and expressions	142
Expressions with 'avoir'	142
Expressions with 'faire'	142
Weather expressions	142
Adjectives	143
'Ce', 'cette', 'ces'	143
'Celui', 'celle', 'ceux', 'celles'	144
'La mien', 'la mienne', etc.	144
'Mon', 'ma', 'mes'	144
'Du', 'de la', 'des'	144
'Au', 'à la', 'aux'	145
Expressions with parts of the body	145
Useful adjectives	145
Adverbs	146
The present participle	147
Expressions of place & position	147
Greetings, exclamations, etc.	147
Vocabulary under topic headings	148
Advice on examinations	153

DOSSIER 1

A LA MAISON

READING COMPREHENSION

1

**A VENDRE
BEL APPARTEMENT**

dans petit immeuble
tout confort
cuisine, 2 chambres, salle de bains,
salle séjour, terrasse, barbecue,
parking, front de mer

PRIX: 350 000F

a Is this flat for sale or to let?
b Is the flat in a house, a small block, or a large block?
c How many bedrooms are there in the flat?
d Which of the following does the flat not have: a terrace; a garage; a barbecue; a dining room?
e What are you told about the position of the flat?
f The price in pounds is about:
   £3 500; £35 000; £350 000.

2

CHAMPIGNY: Av. du Parc

Belle villa, agréable jardin, petit verger,
salle-séjour avec cheminée rustique,
trois chambres, deux salles de bains,
cuisine, sous-sol, garage, chauffage mazout

a As well as a garden, what extra land does the house have?
b What is specially attractive about the living room?
c As well as the usual rooms, what extra space does the house have?
d How is the house heated?

3

**MEDITERRANEE:
PROPRIETAIRE
POUR 139.000F**

RÉSERVEZ AVEC SEULEMENT 5.000F

Demandez notre documentation.
Téléphonez-nous.
Venez nous voir dans nos bureaux.

PORT-BARCARÈS

Ouvert de 9 h à 19 h tous les jours y compris dimanches et jours fériés.

TÉL:
(68) 86.12.15
(68) 86.20.15

A PARIS 31, RUE DE RIVOLI 75004. TÉL: (1) 277.11.13.

BON A RETOURNER A MERLIN
4, AVENUE DE PARIS – 94300 VINCENNES

Sans engagement de ma part, envoyez-moi votre documentation gratuite sur vos programmes.

NOM ....
ADDRESS ....
.... TÉL ....

a How much deposit must you pay for one of these flats?
b Is the price quoted for a flat the highest price or the lowest price?
c When are the firm's offices open? Give as much detail as possible
d What will you get if you send in the reply coupon?
e How much must you pay for what you will receive?

4

Cher David

Merci pour ta lettre. Je suis très content d'avoir un correspondant anglais. Tu me demandes de décrire où j'habite. Eh bien voilà.

J'habite un HLM au neuvième étage d'un grand immeuble moderne. Mon appartement est grand. Il y a un salon, une salle à manger, trois chambres, une cuisine et une salle de bains. Dans la salle à manger il y a une grande table, six chaises et un buffet. Au salon, il y a le poste de télévision, trois fauteuils confortables, un long canapé et une petite table. Dans le vestibule se trouvent des placards, une glace et le téléphone.

Ma soeur Françoise, qui a neuf ans, joue dans le vestibule pendant que je fais mes devoirs dans ma chambre. Quand il fait beau, elle joue sur le balcon. Maman prépare les repas dans la cuisine, et nous prenons le petit déjeuner à la cuisine. Mais le soir et les weekends on mange dans la salle à manger. Papa aide maman, surtout les weekends. Le soir, Françoise met le couvert et moi, je fais la vaisselle. Mon petit frère Antoine n'aide pas. C'est un bébé. Il a un an.

Je dois finir cette lettre maintenant, car maman m'appelle. Ecris-moi bientôt,

Alain

a In what type of flat does Alain live?
b On which floor is Alain's flat situated?
c Name **three** items of furniture that are in the dining room and **three** that are in the lounge.
d In which two places does Françoise play?
e Where does Alain do his homework?
f Where does the family have breakfast?
g When do they eat in the dining room?
h How does Alain help his mother?
i Who lays the table?
j Why does Antoine not help?

5

Chère Sandra

Merci pour ta gentille lettre. Je m'excuse de ne pas t'avoir répondu, mais j'ai été très occupée. Nous avons déménagé il y a quinze jours, et nous avons beaucoup à faire dans la nouvelle maison.

Elle est très jolie, cette maison. Au rez-de-chaussée il y a un vestibule, la salle à manger, le salon et la cuisine. Dans le vestibule se trouvent un portemanteau, une glace et le téléphone. Dans la salle à manger il y a une grande table ronde, un petit buffet et six chaises. J'aime le grand salon où se trouvent un poste de télévision, trois fauteuils confortables, une petite table, un long canapé, une cheminée, beaucoup de peintures au mur, deux grandes fenêtres et une porte qui donne sur le jardin. Maman travaille dans la cuisine où elle fait cuire tous nos repas. Il y a un réfrigérateur un lave-vaisselle, une cuisinière à gaz et plusieurs casseroles sur des étagères. Le congélateur est trop grand pour mettre à la cuisine, il est dans le garage.

Au premier étage il y a trois chambres et la salle de bains. Maman et papa ont une grande chambre avec un balcon. Ma chambre est plus petite, mais très jolie, avec une grande fenêtre qui donne sur le jardin. La chambre d'amis est à côté de la mienne. C'est là que tu dormiras quand tu viendras chez moi pendant les vacances!

Ecris-moi bientôt,
Bons baisers

Nicole

a Où est la grande table ronde?
b Est-ce que le téléphone est dans le salon?
c Que fait la mère de Nicole dans la cuisine?
d Est-ce que Nicole regarde la télévision dans la salle à manger?
e Combien de fauteuils y a-t-il dans le salon?
f Comment est le buffet?
g Combien de pièces y a-t-il au premier étage?
h Où est la porte qui donne sur le jardin?
i Où se trouve la chambre d'amis?
j Pourquoi le congélateur est-il dans le garage?

6

Marcel Pagnol is a writer well-known in France for his novels, plays, and film scripts. The following extract is taken from his book *La Gloire de mon Père* in which he recalls happy memories of his childhood in Provence.

◀ Alors commencèrent les plus beaux jours de ma vie. La maison s'appelait La Bastide Neuve, mais elle était neuve depuis bien longtemps. C'était une ancienne ferme en ruine, restaurée trente ans plus tôt par un monsieur de la ville. Mon père et mon oncle lui payaient un loyer de 80 francs par an, que leurs femmes trouvaient un peu exagéré.

Il y avait au rez-de-chaussée une immense salle à manger avec une petite cheminée en marbre véritable. Un escalier menait aux quatre chambres du premier étage. Les fenêtres de ces chambres avaient des espèces de volets sur lesquels était tendue une fine toile métallique pour arrêter les insectes de la nuit.

L'éclairage était assuré par des lampes à pétrole, et quelques bougies de secours. Mais comme nous prenions tous nos repas sur la terrasse il y avait aussi la lampe-tempête. Chaque soir, mon père l'allumait. Dès qu'on la suspendait à une branche, elle était entourée d'un nuage de papillons dont les ombres dansaient un moment sur la nappe, puis les pauvres bêtes tombaient toutes cuites dans nos assiettes. ▶

EITHER:
Translate the passage into English.
OR:
Answer the following questions:

a What does the author mean when he says 'elle était neuve depuis bien longtemps.'?
b How long ago was the house renovated?
c What did the wives think of the amount of rent paid?
d How were insects prevented from flying in through the bedroom windows?
e Which **two** types of lighting were there indoors?
f What happened to the moths that gathered round the storm lantern?

LISTENING COMPREHENSION

1

You are going to hear three people talking about where they live. Listen carefully before answering in English the following questions:

Françoise

a How old is Françoise?
b Where exactly is her bedsit?
c Name the **two** important amenities which her flat does not have.
d How does she do her cooking?
e Where can she eat for ten francs?
f Where are the toilets situated?
g Besides a bed, table and chair, what other furniture does she have in her bedsit?
h What **two** things has she done to improve the appearance of her room?

Alain

a What does Alain do for a living?
b How many children does he have and what are their ages?

5

c In what type of accommodation do they live?
d Where is Aulnay?
e Where do they eat their meals?
f At what time does Monsieur Reymond leave home in the morning?
g Which **two** types of public transport does he use?
h How long does his journey to work take?
i What does he do after the evening meal?

Christiane

a How old is Christiane?
b How many are there in her family and who are they?
c On which floor is their flat situated?
d What and where is La Défense?
e How long have they been living there?
f Give **two** reasons why she likes their flat.
g What unfortunate event occurred last year?
h Where are the shops?
i What does her mother say about the shops?

2

A strange evening in a farmhouse

Listen carefully to the passage before answering in English the following questions:

a Name **three** things the writer ate for supper.
b How was the room lit?
c What were the writer's feelings about Geneviève?
d What did he do later?
e Give **two** facts about the weather at this time.
f What building did he visit?
g What noise did he hear there?
h On returning home, where did he go first?
i Where did he then go, and how did he get there?
j What are you told about the way in which this room was lit?
k What did the writer notice, and what was particularly strange about it?
l After taking a step forward, who or what did he find, and where?

GRAMMAR EXERCISES

1

Write the following sentences putting the verb in brackets into the present tense:

a Je (s'appeler) Chantal.
b Elle (se lever) à huit heures.
c Nous (dire) 'Bonjour' à nos amis.
d Vous (écrire) à vos parents.
e Le samedi, on (aller) au cinéma.
f Mes grands-parents (venir) nous voir chaque semaine.
g Les enfants (faire) leurs devoirs.
h Philippe (prendre) un bain.
i Ils (avoir) une jolie maison au bord de la mer.
j Il (mettre) son stylo dans sa poche.

2

Copy out the passage below, putting each verb in brackets into the correct form. You will need to use the present tense and the imperative.

Ce soir, Monsieur et Madame Lebrun (aller) au cinéma. Avant de partir, Madame Lebrun (dire) à ses deux filles Madeleine et Marianne:
‹(Faire) vos devoirs, (jouer) avec votre petit frère, n'(oublier) pas de donner à manger au chien, et (aller) au lit à dix heures.›
Maintenant il (être) huit heures. Madeleine (faire) ses devoirs, et Marianne (jouer) avec le petit Antoine. Une demi-heure plus tard, Antoine (se coucher), Madeleine (donner) à manger au chien, et puis les deux soeurs (regarder) la télévision jusqu'à dix heures.
Marianne (aller) se coucher, mais Madeleine (dire):
‹Je ne (vouloir) pas me coucher, je (aller) lire.›
A onze heures Monsieur et Madame Lebrun (revenir) du cinéma.
‹Comment!› (crier) Madame Lebrun, ‹tu n'(être) pas au lit!›
‹Non maman,› (expliquer) Madeleine, ‹j'(avoir) mal aux dents et je ne (pouvoir) pas dormir.›
‹Alors,› (répondre) Madame Lebrun, ‹(prendre) une aspirine et (aller) au lit. Demain matin, je (aller) t'emmener chez le dentiste.›
‹Oh non maman, ce n'(être) pas nécessaire! Je n'(avoir) plus mal aux dents!›

TRAVAIL ORAL

1

Make up some sentences about where you live using the tables below:

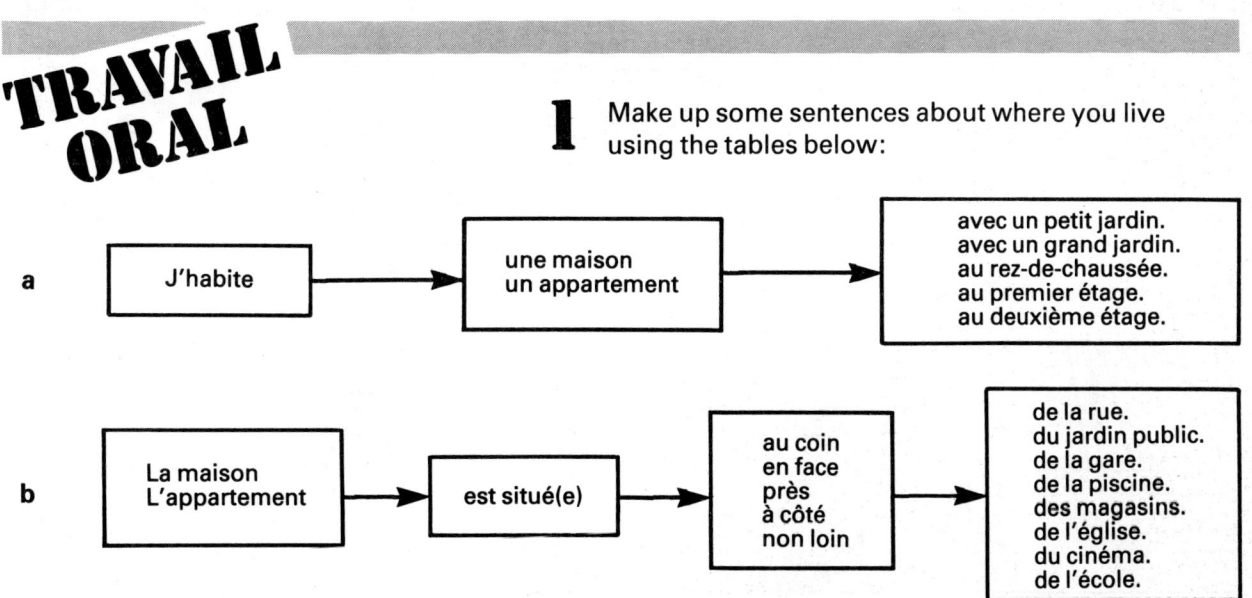

7

2

Look at the picture of the kitchen scene and answer these questions:

a Où sommes-nous dans la maison?
b Quelle est la date au calendrier?
c Combien de placards y a-t-il aux murs?
d Où se trouve l'aspirateur?
e Que boit le chat sous la table?
f Qu'est-ce qu'il y a sur la table au centre de la cuisine? (Nommez quatre objets.)
g Comment est-ce que le garçon aide sa mère?
h Que fait le chien?
i Quelle heure est-il?
j Que fait la petite fille?

3

To do the next exercise you will need to refer to the letter from Nicole which appears on page 4.

Here is the removal van which brought some of the furniture to Nicole's new house. Tell the removal men in which room they should put each piece of furniture. If an item is not mentioned in the text you must decide where it should go.
The first one is done for you:
Mettez la glace dans le vestibule, s'il vous plaît.

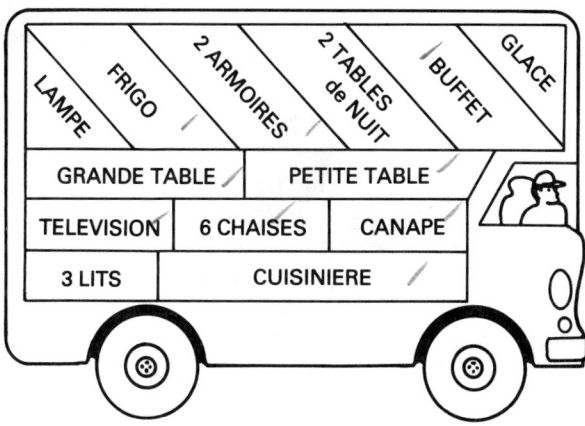

4
SPOT THE DIFFERENCE!

Look carefully at the two following pictures and say what the differences are.

EXAMPLE:
Dans l'image numéro un, il y a trois chaises autour de la table.
Dans l'image numéro deux, il y a deux chaises autour de la table.

You should be able to find at least **ten** more differences.

TRAVAIL ECRIT

1

Write the answers to all the exercises in the TRAVAIL ORAL section.

2

Write a letter to your French penfriend describing your house or flat, giving as much detail as possible. To do this exercise, you will find it useful to refer to the letters which appear in the READING COMPREHENSION.

9

VOCABULARY

Reading comprehension

1
immeuble (*m*) – block of flats
salle (*f*) séjour – living room
 (Note: this is the shortened form of salle de séjour, as used in advertisements)
vendre – to sell

2
chauffage – heating
mazout – oil
sous-sol (*m*) – basement
verger (*m*) – orchard

3
gratuit – free of charge
jour (*m*) férié – public holiday
propriétaire (*m*) – owner

4
aider – to help
balcon (*m*) – balcony
bientôt – soon
buffet (*m*) – sideboard
canapé (*m*) – settee
étage (*m*) – floor, storey
(au premier étage) – on the first floor
faire la vaisselle – to do the washing-up
fauteuil (*m*) – armchair
glace (*f*) – mirror
HLM – French equivalent of English council flat
mettre le couvert – to lay the table
placard (*m*) – cupboard
repas (*m*) – meal
surtout – especially

5
casserole (*f*) – saucepan
chambre (*f*) d'amis – spare bedroom
congélateur (*m*) – freezer
cuisinière (*f*) – cooker
cuire – to cook
déménager – to move house
donner sur – to lead into, to overlook
étagère (*f*) – shelf
il y a – ago
lave-vaisselle (*m*) – dishwasher
occupé – busy
peinture (*f*) – painting
portemanteau (*m*) – coat rack
(au) rez-de- – (on) the ground
 chaussée floor

6
assiette (*f*) – plate
bougie (*f*) – candle
cuit – cooked
dès que – as soon as
éclairage (*m*) – lighting
entouré (de) – surrounded (by)
escalier (*m*) – stairs
espèce (*f*) – sort
ferme (*f*) – farm
loyer (*m*) – rent
nappe (*f*) – tablecloth
neuf [neuve (*f*)] – new
nuage (*m*) – cloud
ombre (*f*) – shadow
papillon (*m*) – butterfly, moth
toile (*f*) – fabric (here, mesh)
volet (*m*) – shutter

Listening comprehension

1
Françoise
affiche (*f*) – poster
chauffage (*m*) – heating
coller – to stick, fasten
étage (*m*) – floor, storey
étudiante (e) – student
fauteuil (*m*) – armchair
immeuble (*m*) – block of flats
lavabo (*m*) – washbasin
meubles (*m pl*) – furniture
(re)peindre – to (re)paint
placard (*m*) – cupboard
réchaud (*m*) – small portable stove
souvent – often
studio (*m*) – bedsit

Alain
banlieue (*f*) – suburb
banque (*f*) – bank
bureau (*m*) – office
chaque – each
employé (*m*) – worker, clerk
fatigué – tired
HLM – French equivalent of English council flat
jardin (*m*) public – park
pareil – same, alike
repas (*m*) – meal
salle (*f*) de séjour – living room
trajet (*m*) – journey
vue (*f*) – view

Christiane
ascenseur (*m*) – lift
cher – dear
cité (*f*) – housing estate
clair – light
depuis – since, for
drôle – funny
pièce (*f*) – room
souterrain – underground
tomber en panne – to break down

2
armoire (*f*) – wardrobe
autour – around
avoir envie (de) – to want, to feel like
bouger – to move
coin (*m*) – corner
se diriger – to go
se dresser – to stand
échelle (*f*) – ladder
écrivain (*m*) – writer
grange (*f*) – barn
grenier (*m*) – attic
lueur (*f*) – gleam
obscur – dark
ombre (*f*) – shadow
orage (*m*) – storm
pas (*m*) – step
pêche (*f*) – peach
pétrole (*f*) – paraffin
sauf – except
se sentir – to feel
seul – alone, lonely
sombre – dark

GRAMMAR

Subject pronouns

A pronoun is a word which replaces a noun. Look at the following examples:

Paul va au collège.	→ Il va au collège.
Paul goes to school.	→ He goes to school.
Marianne achète une robe.	→ Elle achète une robe.
Marianne buys a dress.	→ She buys a dress.
Le livre est sur la table.	→ Il est sur la table.
The book is on the table.	→ It is on the table.
La souris est dans une cage.	→ Elle est dans une cage.
The mouse is in a cage.	→ It is in a cage.

Here are all the subject pronouns in French:
je – I (change to j' before a vowel or a silent 'h')
tu – you (singular)
il – he
elle – she
on – people, they, we (see note at the end of this section)
nous – we
vous – you (singular or plural)*
ils – they (m)
elles – they (f)

*Use of 'tu' and 'vous'

1 'Tu' is used to speak to a child, a member of your family, a friend, or an animal.

2 'Tu' is being increasingly used in French nowadays; in fact, nearly all young French people call each other 'tu' whether they have met before or not.

3 'Vous' is the plural of 'tu'. If you speak to both your parents, or to several friends, at the same time, you will say 'vous'.

4 'Vous' is also used in the singular, as a more formal way of speaking to someone. You would use it to speak to a stranger, someone you did not know very well and, if you are a child or young person, you would use 'vous' to address any adult, other than a member of your family. This means, therefore, that your French teacher may well call you 'tu' but you will speak to your teacher as 'vous'.

The pronoun 'il'

This can be used in what is called an 'impersonal' way.
We can use 'il' when we wish to describe the weather.
EXAMPLE:
il fait beau, il pleut (See page 142 for full list.)
OTHER USES:
il y a – there is **or** there are
il faut – it is necessary
il vaut mieux – it is better

Reflexive pronouns

These are:
me – myself
te – yourself
se – himself, herself, itself
nous – ourselves
vous – yourself, yourselves
se – themselves

Me, te, and se, become m' t' s' before a vowel or a silent 'h'.

You will see how these pronouns are used by looking at the reflexive verb 'se coucher' in the verb list on page 12.

Use of the pronoun 'on'

- 'On' is an extremely common and useful pronoun in French.
- It takes the 'il' and 'elle' form of the verb.
- It has many different meanings, but it should almost never be translated into English as 'one'.

Look at the examples of its use given below. Now try to find and note others from your reading of this book.

EXAMPLE:
On dit que...   People say that...
             or They say that...

Ici on parle français. — French is spoken here.

On entendait un bruit étrange. — A strange noise was heard.

- In familiar, everyday speech, particularly among young people, 'on' is often used instead of 'nous' to mean 'we'.
EXAMPLE:
On a fait du camping en Bretagne. — We went camping in Brittany.

- NOTE
Si on allait au cinéma? — How about going the cinema?

The present tense

Verbs in French are divided into **three** main groups according to the spelling of the **infinitive** (name) of the verb.
1. —er verbs, e.g. donner – to give
2. —ir verbs, e.g. finir – to finish
3. —re verbs, e.g. vendre – to sell

Most verbs in French form their present tense in a regular way, according to definite rules.
- To form the present tense of all regular verbs, remove the infinitive ending —er, —ir, or —re.
- This leaves what is called the **stem** of the verb.
- To this stem, you add the correct present tense endings.

Given below is the present tense of our three sample verbs, with the endings in heavy type:

```
DONNER
je donne
tu donnes
il/elle/on donne
nous donnons
vous donnez
ils/elles donnent
```

```
VENDRE
je vends
tu vends
il/elle/on vend
nous vendons
nous vendez
ils/elles vendent
```

```
FINIR
je finis
tu finis
il/elle/on finit
nous finissons
vous finissez
ils/elles finissent
```

There is a group of —ir verbs which do not form their present tense in the same way as 'finir', although they are not classed as **irregular** verbs.

The commonest of these verbs are:
courir – to run
dormir – to sleep
partir – to leave
servir – to serve
sortir – to go out

EXAMPLE:
```
partir – to leave
je pars
tu pars
il/elle-on part
nous partons
vous partez
ils/elles partent
```

French also contains a number of **reflexive verbs**. Many of them are regular —er verbs, which form their present tense in the same way as 'donner', but there is an extra, reflexive pronoun to be added.

EXAMPLE:
```
se coucher – to go to bed
je me couche
tu te couches
il/elle/on se couche
nous nous couchons
vous vous couchez
ils/elles se couchent
```

A number of verbs in French do not form their present tense according to the above rules. They are known as **irregular verbs** and must be learnt by heart

aller – to go
je vais – I go, I am going
tu vas
il/elle/on va
nous allons
vous allez
ils/elles vont

écrire – to write
j'écris – I write, I am writing
tu écris
il/elle/on écrit
nous écrivons
vous écrivez
ils/elles écrivent

avoir – to have
j'ai – I have, I am having
tu as
il/elle/on a
nous avons
vous avez
ils/elles ont

être – to be
je suis – I am
tu es
il/elle/on est
nous sommes
vous êtes
ils/elles sont

boire – to drink
je bois – I drink, I am drinking
tu bois
il/elle/on boit
nous buvons
vous buvez
ils/elles boivent

faire – to do, to make
je fais – I do, I am doing
tu fais
il/elle/on fait
nous faisons
vous faites
ils/elles font

devoir – to have to, must
je dois – I have to, I must
tu dois
il/elle/on doit
nous devons
vous devez
ils/elles doivent

lire – to read
je lis – I read, I am reading
tu lis
il/elle/on lit
nous lisons
vous lisez
ils/elles lisent

dire – to say, to tell
je dis – I say, I am saying
tu dis
il/elle/on dit
nous disons
vous dites
ils/elles disent

mettre – to put, to put on
je mets – I put, I am putting
tu mets
il/elle/on met
nous mettons
vous mettez
ils/elles mettent

```
┌──────── ouvrir – to open ────────┐
│   j'ouvre – I open, I am opening  │
│             tu ouvres             │
│          il/elle/on ouvre         │
│            nous ouvrons           │
│            vous ouvrez            │
│          ils/elles ouvrent        │
└───────────────────────────────────┘

┌──────── venir – to come ─────────┐
│   je viens – I come, I am coming  │
│             tu viens              │
│          il/elle/on vient         │
│            nous venons            │
│            vous venez             │
│          ils/elles viennent       │
└───────────────────────────────────┘

┌──── pouvoir – to be able, can ───┐
│    je peux – I can, I am able    │
│             tu peux              │
│          il/elle/on peut         │
│           nous pouvons           │
│            vous pouvez           │
│         ils/elles peuvent        │
└──────────────────────────────────┘

┌──────── vouloir – to want ───────┐
│  je veux – I want, I am wanting  │
│             tu veux              │
│          il/elle/on veut         │
│           nous voulons           │
│            vous voulez           │
│          ils/elles veulent       │
└──────────────────────────────────┘

┌──────── prendre – to take ───────┐
│  je prends – I take, I am taking │
│            tu prends             │
│          il/elle/on prend        │
│           nous prenons           │
│            vous prenez           │
│         ils/elles prennent       │
└──────────────────────────────────┘

┌──────── voir – to see ───────────┐
│   je vois – I see, I am seeing   │
│             tu vois              │
│          il/elle/on voit         │
│           nous voyons            │
│            vous voyez            │
│          ils/elles voient        │
└──────────────────────────────────┘

┌─────── recevoir – to receive ────┐
│ je reçois – I receive, I am receiving │
│            tu reçois             │
│         il/elle/on reçoit        │
│          nous recevons           │
│           vous recevez           │
│         ils/elles reçoivent      │
└──────────────────────────────────┘

┌──────── savoir – to know ────────┐
│  je sais – I know, I am knowing  │
│             tu sais              │
│          il/elle/on sait         │
│           nous savons            │
│            vous savez            │
│          ils/elles savent        │
└──────────────────────────────────┘
```

It is worth remembering that a number of irregular verbs have compounds which are conjugated in the same way.

EXAMPLE:

mettre	remettre – to put back
	admettre – to admit
prendre	comprendre – to understand
	apprendre – to learn, to teach
venir	revenir – to come back
	devenir – to become
tenir	retenir – to book (e.g. seats)
(conjugated like 'venir')	
	maintenir – to maintain

You should make a list of other compounds which you come across in your reading.

Use of the present tense

- As its name suggests, the present tense is used when talking or writing about the present time.

- But there is one extremely important point to remember. In **English**, we have **two** present tenses:

EXAMPLE:
simple present: I give
present continuous: I am giving

In **French**, there is only **one** present tense.

EXAMPLE:
Je donne – I give **and** I am giving

EXAMPLE:
Je fais mes devoirs avant le souper.
I do my homework before supper.

Qu'est-ce que tu fais? Je fais mes devoirs.
What are you doing? I'm doing my homework.

Quel temps fait-il? Il pleut.
What is the weather like? It is raining.

En Bretagne, il pleut souvent.
In Brittany it often rains.

Other points to remember

Verbs such as 'manger', 'nager', 'changer' keep the 'e' before a vowel which would otherwise give a hard 'g'.

EXAMPLE:
nous mangeons; nous nageons; nous changeons

- **Note that this rule applies to other tenses of these verbs.**

Some verbs require a grave accent on an 'e', when it is the final syllable.

EXAMPLE:
j'achète
tu achètes
il/elle/on achète
BUT:
nous achetons
vous achetez
THEN:
ils/elles achètent

SIMILARLY:
je me lève
tu te lèves
il/elle/on se lève
nous nous levons
vous vous levez
ils/elles se lèvent

- Note what happens to the accents in the verb espérer – to hope
j'espère
tu espères
il/elle/on espère
nous espérons
vous espérez
ils/elles espèrent

- Note what happens to the 'y' in verbs such as envoyer – to send, aboyer – to bark
j'envoie
tu envoies
il/elle/on envoie
nous envoyons
vous envoyez
ils/elles envoient

- Note the doubling of a consonant in 'appeler' and 'jeter', je m'appelle, etc.
BUT:
nous nous appelons, vous vous appelez
je jette, etc.
AND:
nous jetons, vous jetez

The imperative

- This is used for giving **orders** or **commands**.
- To do this, use the 'tu' or 'vous' form of the present tense, but without the word 'tu' or 'vous'.
- For —er verbs, leave off the final 's' of the 'tu' form to make the imperative.

EXAMPLE:
Regarde ton livre, Look at your book.
Finissez vos devoirs. Finish your homework.
Attendez ici. Wait here.
Va vite. Go quickly.
Prenez vos cahiers. Take your exercise books.

- Note the imperative forms for reflexive verbs.

    EXAMPLE:
    Lève-toi.   Get up.
    Asseyez-vous.   Sit down.

- The 'nous' form of the present tense may also be used on its own as a type of imperative, for making suggestions.

    EXAMPLE:
    Partons tout de suite.   Let's leave at once.
    Allons à la plage.   Let's go to the beach.

- The verbs 'avoir' and 'être' have irregular imperative forms:

avoir	*être*
aie	sois
ayons	soyons
ayez	soyez

    EXAMPLE:
    N'aie pas peur.   Don't be afraid.
    Sois sage.   Be good.
    Soyez raisonnable.   Be reasonable.

DOSSIER 2
LA FAMILLE ET
LES AMIS

READING COMPREHENSION

1

Paul and Marc were schoolfriends, but Marc and his family have now moved away from the district. However, the two boys still write to each other.

Jaunay, 13 novembre

Cher Marc,

Merci pour ta dernière lettre, que j'ai reçue il y a trois jours.

Enfin j'ai un moment pour t'écrire. J'ai beaucoup à faire ces jours-ci. Cette semaine je joue dans la finale du tournoi de tennis de table à l'école. Jeudi, il y a un match de football contre le lycée Brasseur. Samedi prochain c'est l'anniversaire de Sylvie et il y a une surprise partie chez elle. Et j'ai beaucoup de devoirs maintenant que je suis en troisième. Les maths surtout je trouve ça très difficile.

Ma soeur Lise va se marier l'été prochain. Son fiancé, Jacques est très sympa. Il est ingénieur. Mon cousin Alain (tu te rappelles? son père, mon oncle Jérome, nous emmenait quelquefois à la pêche) travaille maintenant dans un garage. Il ne gagne pas beaucoup pendant son apprentissage, mais au moins il est sûr d'avoir un emploi à la fin.

Moi, je ne sais pas encore ce que je veux faire après mes examens, mais surtout je ne veux pas travailler dans un bureau. Ça doit être pire que l'école!

Maman dit que si tu veux venir passer quelques jours chez nous pendant les vacances tu n'as qu'à le dire.

Amitiés,

Paul

---

a In which **two** sports fixtures is Paul involved during this week?
b What is happening next Saturday?
c When is his sister getting married?
d What does her fiancé do for a living?
e Why might Marc remember Paul's uncle Jérome?
f What is Alain doing now?
g What does Paul say about his own plans for a job?
h What message does Paul's mother send to Marc?

2

LES SOUPES MAGGI
POTAGE DE LEGUMES AU VERMICELLE

Préparation pour 1 litre de potage; quatre assiettes

1. Versez lentement le contenu du sachet dans un litre d'eau bouillante.
2. Remuez à l'aide d'un fouet pour bien mélanger.
3. Couvrez partiellement et laissez cuire à feu doux pendant dix minutes en remuant de temps en temps.

a Is this a meat or vegetable soup?
b How many servings does the packet provide?
c Should you use hot or cold water?
d What is the second step in making the soup?
e Should it be cooked covered or uncovered?
f Should it be cooked over a low heat or a high heat?

3

UNE RECETTE DE TANTE MARTHE
SALADE PROVENÇALE

Préparez quatre oeufs durs, coupez deux belles tomates et une grosse betterave. Lavez une petite laitue. Dans un saladier en verre transparent de préférence, mettez dans le fond les feuilles de laitue. Posez par-dessus quelques quartiers d'oeufs durs, les morceaux de tomates et de betterave. Sur le dessus faites une décoration avec les oeufs durs qui vous restent, et préparez à part une vinaigrette.
Pour la Vinaigrette: Dans un bol mettez un peu de moutarde, deux cuillerées de vinaigre, six cuillerées d'huile d'olive, salez et poivrez, ajoutez un peu d'ail écrasé.
Au moment de servir, arrosez la salade avec la vinaigrette.

a What sort of eggs do you need for this recipe?
b Name the **three** other ingredients of the salad.
c What is the best sort of salad bowl to use?
d How should you decorate the top of the salad?
e How many spoonfuls of vinegar do you need for the vinaigrette dressing?
f What must you do to the garlic before adding it?

4
MEMORIES OF A COUNTRY CHILDHOOD

Pierre Poivre recalls his childhood in a village in southern France. Here he explains why Sunday was his favourite day.

◀ J'aimais les dimanches – surtout en été. Mon grand-père avait une petite maison de campagne, entourée de vignes, à quatre kilomètres du village, et le dimanche on y allait, toute la famille, faire une grillade.

D'abord, il fallait préparer ça. Après le petit déjeuner, vers neuf heures et demie, j'allais à la boulangerie acheter un gros gâteau. C'était seulement le dimanche qu'on mangeait du gâteau, parce que les gâteaux coûtent cher en France. Maman et mes deux soeurs préparaient la viande – le plus souvent c'était du poulet, du canard, ou du lapin, et des salades. Mon père et mon oncle Philippe descendaient en voiture à la maison de campagne préparer le feu. Ils prenaient avec eux plusieurs bouteilles de vin, un panier plein d'escargots, et des sarments (ce sont de petites branches de vigne) pour faire le feu.

Vers onze heures, ma tante Françoise arrivait chez nous – elle apportait toujours du saucisson, du fromage et des fruits. Alors, maman, mes soeurs, mon cousin Pascal, et moi montions dans la voiture de tante Françoise pour rejoindre mon père et mon oncle. Je me rappelle que ma tante ne conduisait pas très bien – elle parlait trop!

En arrivant, on dressait une grande table sous les arbres dans le jardin, et puis on allumait le feu. Que c'était beau! Vers midi et demi, mes grands-parents arrivaient et on passait à table. D'abord, on mangeait des escargots, avec de la mayonnaise. Il fallait faire attention, car on tenait les escargots avec les doigts, et ils étaient très chauds. On les sortait de leurs coquilles avec de petites fourchettes que maman apportait exprès pour ça. Ensuite, il y avait du saucisson. A la maison je ne mangeais jamais de saucisson, mais quand c'était fait sur la grillade c'était délicieux.

Puis, papa et l'oncle Philippe retournaient à leur feu pour faire cuire la viande. Nous, les enfants, allions jouer un peu, pendant que ma mère, ma tante, et mes grands-parents bavardaient.

Un quart d'heure ou vingt minutes plus tard mon père criait: ‹A table, les enfants!› et on mangeait le poulet ou le lapin avec de la salade et des pommes de terre. Puis, il y avait du fromage, des fruits, et pour finir le gâteau. Bien sûr, avec tout ça, les grandes personnes buvaient du vin. A nous, les enfants, on donnait un peu de vin et nous allions remplir nos verres d'eau de la source au fond du jardin.

Après, nous allions pêcher des goujons dans la rivière pendant que les grandes personnes prenaient le café et causaient. Je crois vraiment que ces dimanches d'été étaient les plus beaux jours de ma vie. ▶

a Give **two** facts about the grandfather's country cottage.
b Why did they eat cake only on Sunday?
c Name **three** types of meat they might have for Sunday lunch.
d What **three** things did the father and uncle take with them?
e What **three** things did Aunt Françoise bring?
f How many people travelled in Aunt Françoise's car, and who were they?
g What does the writer say about Aunt Françoise's driving?
h At what time did the grandparents arrive?
i Give **two** facts you are told about eating snails.
j What does the author say about eating sausage?
k About how long did it take the author's father and uncle to cook the meat?
l Name **two** other items they ate before the cake.
m Explain exactly what the children drank.
n What did the children do after the meal?
o What **two** things did the adults do after the meal?

5

Le dernier jour des vacances

A group of four young people from Paris have been spending their holiday camping at La Franqui, a small seaside resort on the Mediterranean coast. Now, it is their last day . . .

JEAN-FRANÇOIS	C'est le dernier jour. Qu'est-ce qu'on fait?
CHANTAL	Mais c'est évident! On va à la plage.
PAUL	Moi, je voudrais bien aller à l'étang chercher des huîtres. Les dernières étaient si bonnes! Tu viens avec moi, Hélène?
HELENE	Non merci. Il y a trop de moustiques. J'ai des piqûres partout.
CHANTAL	Moi aussi.
JEAN-FRANÇOIS	Bon alors. Ce matin Paul va aux huîtres et nous, on va à la plage. Mais d'abord je dois réparer ma planche à voile. La voile est un peu déchirée. Tu me donnes un coup de main Chantal?
CHANTAL	Oui, bien sûr.
JEAN-FRANÇOIS	Et cet après-midi? Si on allait à Collioure?
HELENE	Oh oui, bonne idée! C'est si joli là-bas. Tu te rappelles, Chantal? La dernière fois qu'on y est allé, il faisait tellement beau!
PAUL	Mais non. Il pleuvait, n'est-ce pas Chantal?
CHANTAL	Je ne me rappelle pas.
JEAN-FRANÇOIS	J'ai l'impression qu'il faisait un temps plutôt gris.
HELENE	Oh, ne discutez pas! Qu'est-ce que ça peut faire? Moi, je veux bien aller à Collioure. Je pourrai acheter un cadeau pour maman. Il y a de belles choses au marché sur le port à Collioure.
CHANTAL	Oui, mais c'est plutôt cher.
HELENE	Oh, tant pis. Tu sais, pour une fois . . .
JEAN-FRANÇOIS	Alors, d'accord pour Collioure. Et ce soir? On va au cinéma?
PAUL	Ah non, pas ça! Je déteste ces petits cinémas de camping.
CHANTAL	Paul a raison. On peut aller au cinéma toute l'année à Paris. C'est bête de perdre son temps à faire ça ici.
HELENE	Mais c'est évident ce qu'on doit faire ce soir! Vous n'avez pas vu l'affiche? Il y a une grande sardinade au camping. Il faut y aller. On s'amusera bien.
PAUL	Oh, tu sais, la dernière sardinade, ce n'était pas si fameux que ça. Trois sardines et un demi-verre de vin rouge pour douze francs – ce n'est pas donné.
HELENE	Ecoute, ce n'était pas si mauvais que ça. Toi, tu étais de mauvaise humeur, Paul, parce que tu avais mal au ventre et que tu n'osais pas manger davantage.
PAUL	Bon alors, ce soir c'est la sardinade. Mais moi, je vais manger une pizza avant d'y aller – je ne veux pas crever de faim!
JEAN-FRANÇOIS	Alors, tout est arrangé. Allons enfants de la patrie, on y va?

a What does Paul want to do in the morning?
b Why does Hélène not wish to go with him?
c What does Jean-François ask Chantal to do?
d What are the **three** different statements made about the weather at Collioure?
e Why does Hélène want to go to Collioure?

f Where exactly is the market?
g What is Chantal's objection to the market?
h Why does Paul not want to go to the cinema?
i Why does Chantal agree with him?
j How does Hélène know about the 'sardinade'?
k What is Paul's complaint about the last 'sardinade'?
l According to Hélène, what sort of mood was Paul in that evening, and why?
m What is Paul going to do this time before the 'sardinade', and why?

d How do we know that Ferdinand was short-sighted?
e What was Joseph pretending to do?
f What was Joseph actually doing?
g What **two** things was the author doing?
h How many children were there in the family?

7

An anxious mother gives instructions to her children

6

The passages which follow are taken from *Le Notaire du Havre* by Georges Duhamel. This novel gives a vivid picture of the life of a lower middle class family in France during the early part of this century.

◀ Dans la salle à manger, brûlait, dès le crépuscule, notre grosse lampe de cuivre, toujours un peu moite de pétrole. Nous venions travailler et jouer là, sous cette lumière enchantée. Maman, pour disposer les assiettes du couvert, repoussait en grondant nos cahiers et nos livres.

Ferdinand traçait des lettres avec soin. Il écrivait, le nez sur la page. Il avait déjà grand besoin de lunettes. On ne s'en aperçut que plus tard. Joseph, les coudes sur la table, faisait semblant de répéter ses leçons, mais il lisait le journal posé devant lui, contre un verre. Cécile jouait sous la table et, de temps en temps, cessant de réciter ‹huit fois huit› et ‹huit fois neuf›, je lui donnais des coups de pied. Nous entendions maman remuer une casserole dans la cuisine, de l'autre côté du mur.

Joseph baîlla vigoureusement, à plusieurs reprises, et cria: ‹On a faim!› ▶

EITHER:
  Translate the passages into English.
OR:
  Answer the following questions:
a How was the room lit?
b Why did the children's mother have to move their books?
c What was Ferdinand doing?

◀ La rue est faite pour qu'on y passe, mes enfants, et non pour qu'on y joue. Ne vous attardez jamais dans la rue, je vous en supplie. Et méfiez-vous de tout. Méfiez-vous des taxis et des camions qui écrasent chaque jour à Paris beaucoup de petits enfants. Méfiez-vous des chiens. Méfiez-vous des ivrognes. Méfiez-vous des gens que vous ne connaissez pas, et si quelqu'un vous adresse la parole, répondez poliment: ‹Oui, monsieur, Non, monsieur› et sauvez-vous sans en avoir l'air. ▶

Answer in English the following questions:
a What is the street not meant for?
b Why must the children beware of taxis and lorries?
c Name **two** types of people that the children must beware of.
d State **two** things the children must do if a stranger should speak to them.

Rewrite the instructions as though the mother were speaking to one child only. To do this you should use the 'tu' form of each verb.

22

8

The passage which follows is taken from the novel *Mon Oncle* by Robert Carrière. The novel is based on a French film of the same name, which featured a famous comic actor called Jacques Tati. Here, the author recalls his own childhood.

◀ Nous avions une maison moderne, avec un petit jardin. Mon père avait l'habitude d'admirer ce jardin le matin, avant le départ pour l'usine. Il restait immobile, sur le perron, le ventre étincelant d'une chaîne de montre et de quatre stylos.

Mes parents étaient gentils, à leur façon. J'avais tout ce qu'un petit garçon pouvait désirer – un beau cartable en cuir, une belle chambre avec un bureau verni, des jouets automatiques qui n'avaient pas besoin de moi pour marcher. Je les mettais en mouvement et ils s'amusaient tout seuls. J'avais aussi des vêtements propres, des chaussures solides, une alimentation excellente.

Chaque matin, mon père me déposait devant l'école. Pendant que je bouclais mon cartable, pendant que mon père, sur le perron, allumait sa première cigarette, ma mère astiquait avec frénésie tout ce qui passait à la portée de sa main.

Nous partions à la même heure, chaque jour. Je m'asseyais à côté de mon père et notre chien montait à l'arrière. C'était un petit teckel qui s'appelait Daki. Quelquefois, il s'échappait la nuit; il partait à la rencontre de trois ou quatre chiens vagabonds, puis, le matin venu, il rentrait couvert de boue, rempli d'odeurs. Ensuite, ma mère le baignait. Il n'aimait pas ça.

La voiture s'ébranlait doucement, traversait le jardin. Quand nous commencions à prendre de la vitesse je me retournais quelquefois. Devant la grille, ma mère agitait, comme un mouchoir d'adieu, son torchon plein de poussière. ▶

Answer in French the following questions:
a Que faisait le père tous les matins avant d'aller à l'usine?
b Qu'est-ce que l'auteur avait dans sa chambre?
c Comment est-ce que l'auteur allait à l'école?
d Que faisait son père sur le perron?
e Où l'auteur s'asseyait-il?
f Qui était à l'arrière?
g Que faisait le chien quelquefois la nuit?
h Comment était-il en rentrant?
i Que faisait la mère ensuite?
j Que faisait la mère devant la grille?

Answer in English the following questions:
a Where did the author's father work?
b Why did his father's stomach shine?
c What does the author say about his toys?
d What do you learn about the author's mother?
e What was the author doing in the morning whilst his father smoked a cigarette?
f In what state did the dog return from his night-time wanderings?
g To what does the author compare his mother shaking her duster?

Translate into English from 'Chaque matin . . .' to the end of the passage.

23

LISTENING COMPREHENSION

1

Paul, a young mechanic, telephones his friend, Madeleine. Listen carefully to their conversation before answering in English the following questions:

a What is Paul's first question when he knows it is Madeleine on the telephone?
b For how long did Madeleine wait for him the previous evening?
c Explain exactly why Paul was late.
d Where were they supposed to meet last Thursday?
e Where did they plan to meet on Saturday and how late was Paul in arriving?
f Why was Madeleine particularly annoyed about his lateness on Sunday?
g How late did he arrive on her birthday?
h What was the reason for his being late?
i Why exactly does Madeleine say she is not planning to go to the disco tomorrow?
j What **two** things does Paul intend to do at home tomorrow before meeting Madeleine?
k Why does he change the time of their meeting?
l What, according to Madeleine, is the advantage of the television?

2

COURRIER DU COEUR

The following letters were written to Mireille, the presenter of a radio programme for young people.
Listen to the letters – and Mireille's replies, before answering in English the following questions:

Claudette

a State **two** things Claudette likes doing.
b What is her problem?
c How long has she had this problem?
d What does she do to try to solve it?
Reply
e What does Mireille say Claudette must not do?
f State **two** things she says Claudette should do.
g How does she try to console Claudette?

Frédéric

a How old is Frédéric?

b State **three** things he says about his appearance.
c What question does he ask?
Reply
d Which quality does Mireille say he has?

Danielle

a What will Danielle do in three months' time?
b Why does she want to find a job?
c Why is she writing to Mireille?
Reply
d Why does Mireille say Danielle is lucky?
e Name **three** places where she might find a job.
f What should she do to find employment?

Jean-Paul

a How old is Jean-Paul?
b How do you know that he is a good pupil at school?
c What rule does his parents make about:
   (i) his going out in the evenings?
   (ii) his having friends home?
d Why is he not allowed to play his records?
e What other complaint does he make?
f What does he want to do?
Reply
g What does Mireille tell Jean-Paul not to do?
h What suggestion does she make about his records?
i What is her comment about pocket money?

GRAMMAR EXERCISES

1

Join the following pairs of sentences together by using 'qui' or 'que':

a Je vais prendre le train.
   Le train part à six heures.
b C'est l'homme.
   J'ai vu l'homme hier.
c La jeune fille porte un pullover rouge.
   Elle habite près de chez moi.
d Les deux garçons jouent au football.
   Les garçons sont mes cousins.
e Je vois cette jeune fille tous les jours.
   Elle s'appelle Annette.
f Le pullover est rouge et noir.
   J'ai acheté le pullover.

2

Make the following sentences negative, using the expression in brackets:

a Il a de l'argent. (ne . . . pas)
b Je sors avant midi. (ne . . . jamais)
c Nous avons vu. (ne . . . personne)
d J'ai remarqué. (ne . . . rien)
e Elle travaille. (ne . . . plus)
f Il a trois francs. (ne . . . que)
g J'ai du pain et du beurre. (ne . . . ni . . . ni . . .)

3

In the passage below, Chantal Lefèvre, a shop assistant in Paris, recalls her childhood in the country.
Write out the passage, putting each verb in brackets into the correct form of the imperfect tense.

 Quand j'(être) petite nous (habiter) en Normandie. Mes grands-parents (avoir) une ferme à trente kilomètres de Rouen. Mes parents (habiter) tout près, avec ma soeur et moi, bien entendu, et mon père (travailler) avec mon grand-père à la ferme. On n'(avoir) pas beaucoup d'argent, on ne (prendre) jamais de vacances, mais nous (être) heureux quand même. J'(aimer) donner à manger aux poules et aux lapins. Quelquefois, ma soeur et moi, nous (faire) la cuisine pendant que maman (aider) papa aux champs. Jeudi, c'(être) jour de marché. On (se lever) très tôt, en hiver il (faire) encore noir. Je (mettre) mon gros manteau et tout le monde (monter) dans le vieux camion de mon grand-père, et nous (partir) pour Rouen. Au marché, nous (vendre) des légumes, des fruits, des fleurs. Après, les hommes (aller) au café boire un verre, mais maman, ma soeur et moi, nous (faire) des courses. Puis, nous (dîner) tous ensemble en ville, et quelquefois mon père nous (emmener) au cinéma. Nous (rentrer) assez tard. Moi, je (s'endormir) souvent en route. En ce temps-là, la vie (être) belle!

TRAVAIL ORAL

1

Que faisiez-vous entre sept heures trente et huit heures moins le quart?

A burglary took place at the Lescures' house last week. All the family were there, but they were all so busy no one heard the burglar.
Inspector Dubois wants to know what they were all doing, and where, between 7.30 p.m. and 7.45 p.m.
Give each person's reply. There is a picture and a **word or phrase** to help you with each one.

(a) Monsieur Lescure — **lire le journal**

(b) Madame Lescure — **regarder la télévision**

(c) Amélie — **faire un gâteau**

(d) Madame Bontemps (soeur de Mme. Lescure) — **tricoter**

(e) Philippe — **faire ses devoirs**

(f) Nicolas — **faire la vaisselle**

(g) Josyane — **téléphoner**

(h) le petit Roger — **dormir**

(i) *Noiraud le chien — **ronger un os**

(j) *Minou le chat — **chasser une souris**

*You will have to use 'il' for these — they can't speak for themselves.

26

2

Que faisiez-vous entre midi et midi et quart?

This time Inspector Dubois is investigating a daring daylight robbery at a jeweller's in the Place de la République. He asks some possible witnesses what they were doing, and where, at the relevant time. Answer for them. Once again, there is a picture clue and a **phrase** for each one.

Monsieur Chiroz homme d'affaires   **lire des documents**

Monsieur et Madame Jack Smith, (touristes)
boire une tasse de café

Jacques Rochefort, représentant
garer la voiture

Madame Lepic   **attendre l'autobus**

Madame Boisvert, boulangère   **servir une cliente**

Pierre Servan, garçon de café
prendre des commandes

Sylvie Boisvert, lycéenne
manger une glace

Robert Daron, lycéen
bavarder avec un copain

Paul Petit, facteur
porter le courrier

Philippe Daudet, mécanicien
réparer une voiture

27

3

Quand j'avais dix ans . . .

Choose one of the following picture series to say what you used to do when you were ten years old. Remember to use the imperfect tense.

First series

Second series

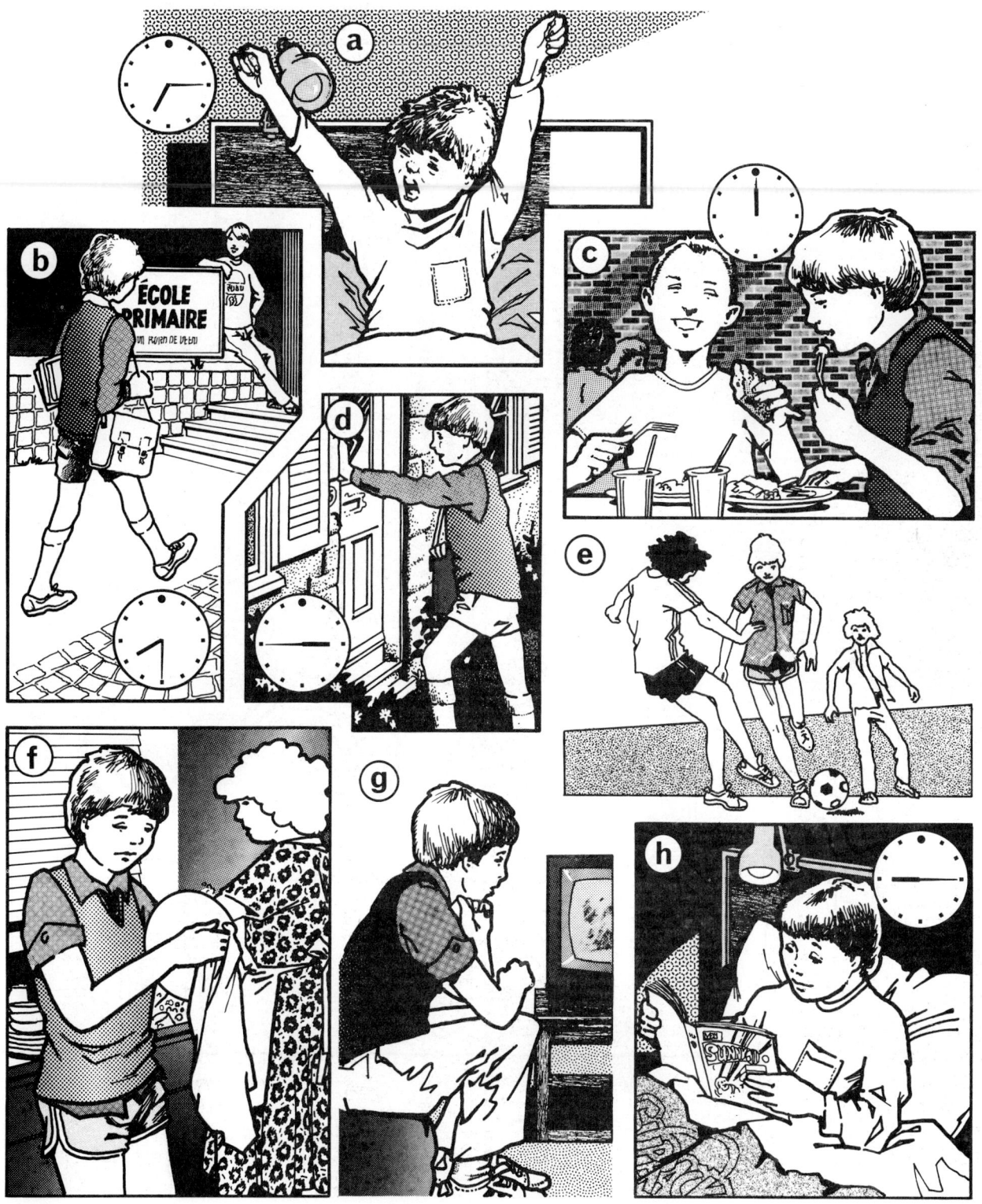

TRAVAIL ECRIT

1

Refer to TRAVAIL ORAL exercises 1 and 2.
Write down people's replies as Inspector Dubois would have written them in his report.
EXAMPLE:
Monsieur Lescure lisait le journal dans le salon.

2

You are Madame Souzay, and you are seventy-three years old.
The pictures below show what you used to do when you were young. Write a sentence about each picture, beginning **'Quand j'étais jeune . . .'** or **'Quand j'avais vingt ans . . .'**

3

Now do the same for Monsieur Souzay.

4

Write a paragraph (*50/60 words*) beginning
EITHER:
   '**Quand j'étais à l'école primaire . . .**'
OR:
   '**Quand j'étais petit(e) . . .**'

5

Write a story which the pictures below suggest to you

VOCABULARY

Reading comprehension

1
anniversaire (m) – birthday
contre – against
emmener – to take (people)
emploi (m) – job
gagner – to earn
ingénieur (m) – engineer
se marier – to get married
oncle (m) – uncle
pêche (f) – fishing
pire – worse
prochain – next
quelquefois – sometimes
se rappeler – to remember
reçu(e) – received
　(from recevoir – to receive)
sûr – sure, certain
surtout – especially
sympa. (slang) – nice, pleasant
　(short for sympathique)
tournoi (m) – tournament

2
à feu doux – on a low heat
bouillant – boiling
contenu (m) – contents
couvrir – to cover
mélanger – to mix
remuer – to stir
verser – to pour

3
ail (m) – garlic
ajouter – to add
betterave (f) – beetroot
bol (m) – bowl
cuillerée – spoonful
écraser – to crush
laitue (f) – lettuce
morceau (m) – piece
moutarde (f) – mustard
oeuf dur (m) – hard-boiled egg
par-dessus – on top
poivrer – to pepper
poser – to put, to place
saler – to salt

4
allumer – to light
au fond de – at the end of
　　at the bottom of
bavarder – to chat
campagne (f) – country
canard (m) – duck
causer – to chat
chaud – hot
conduire – to drive
coquille (f) – shell
coûter – to cost
d'abord – first
doigt (m) – finger
dresser – to put up (a table, a tent, etc.)
entouré – surrounded
escargot (m) – snail
faire attention – to be careful
faire cuire – to cook
feu (m) – fire
fourchette (f) – fork
fromage (m) – cheese
goujon (m) – gudgeon (very small fish)
il fallait – it was necessary
lapin (m) – rabbit
panier (m) – basket
passer à table – to sit down to a meal
pêcher – to fish
peu – little
poulet (m) – chicken
remplir – to fill
saucisson (m) – sausage
seulement – only
source (f) – spring (of water)
souvent – often
surtout – especially
tenir – to hold
trop – too, too much
verre (m) – glass
vers – about
vie (f) – life
voiture (f) – car

5
affiche (f) – poster
bête – stupid
crever – to die (colloquial)
discuter – (here) to argue
étang (m) – pond, pool
fameux – marvellous (colloquial)
gris – grey
huître (f) – oyster
marché (m) – market
moustique (m) – mosquito
oser – to dare
partout – everywhere
piqûre (f) – sting, bite
plage (f) – beach
planche (f) à voile – windsurfing board
plutôt – rather
qu'est-ce que ça peut faire – what does it matter?
réparer – to repair
sardinade (f) – outdoor party, where fresh sardines are cooked on an open fire or barbecue
tant pis – too bad, never mind
tellement – so
ventre (m) – belly
voile (f) – sail

6
s'apercevoir (de) – to notice
à plusieurs reprises – several times
bâiller – to yawn
brûler – to burn
casserole (f) – saucepan
cesser – to stop, to cease
coude (m) – elbow
coup (m) de pied – kick
crépuscule (m) – twilight, dusk
cuivre (m) – copper
faire semblant de – to pretend
moite – moist
soin (m) – care

7
adresser la parole – to speak
s'attarder – to dawdle, to hang about
camion (m) – lorry
écraser – to run over
gens (f pl) – people

ivrogne (*m*) – drunk (person)
se méfier (de) – to beware (of)
se sauver – to run away, to make one's escape

8

agiter – to wave
à leur façon – in their own way
s'asseoir – to sit
astiquer – to polish
avec frénésie – frantically
boucler – to fasten, to do up
boue (*f*) – mud
bureau (*m*) – desk
cartable (*m*) – satchel, school bag
s'ébranler – to start up, to move off (car, train)
s'échapper – to escape
immobile – without moving, still
jouet (*m*) – toy
montre (*f*) – watch
mouchoir (*m*) – handkerchief
odeur (*f*) – smell
perron (*m*) – step, flight of steps
à la portée de la main – within reach
poussière (*f*) – dust
teckel (*m*) – dachshund
torchon (*m*) – duster
usine (*f*) – factory
ventre (*m*) – belly, stomach
verni – varnished
vitesse (*f*) – speed

Listening comprehension

1

ajuster – to adjust
arrêt (*m*) d'autobus – bus stop
attendre – to wait (for)
avoir rendez-vous – to have arranged to meet
ça y est! – that's it!
copain (*m*) – friend, pal
d'accord – agreed, O.K.
douche (*f*) – shower
en avoir assez – to have enough, to be fed up
ensemble – together
faute (*f*) – fault
freins (*m pl*) – brakes
jusqu'à – until
patron (*m*) – boss
piscine (*f*) – swimming-pool
prendre un verre – to have a drink
recommencer – to begin again
supplémentaire – extra
tomber en panne – to break down

2

Claudette
au moins – at least
bientôt – soon
bouton (*m*) – spot
copain (*m*) – friend

copine (*f*) – friend
figure (*f*) – face
maquillage (*m*) – make-up
ne servir à rien – to be no use
oser – to dare
s'en faire – to worry
surtout – above all, especially

Frédéric
gentil (le) – nice, kind
lunettes (*f pl*) – glasses
malgré – in spite of
peut-être – perhaps
ressembler (à) – to look like

Danielle
annonce (*f*) – advertisement
chance (*f*) – luck, fortune
fauché (slang) – broke
s'y prendre – to go about (doing something)
venir de – to have just . . .

Jean-Paul
avoir envie de – to feel like, to want
défendre – to forbid
disque (*m*) – record
s'entendre avec – to get on with
note (*f*) – mark
paraître – to seem
passer – to play (records)
quant à – as for
raisonnable – reasonable
sauf – except
vraiment – really

GRAMMAR

The imperfect tense

The imperfect tense is formed in this way.

Find the 'nous' form of the present tense of the verb you wish to use. Drop the ending —ons, and add the imperfect endings:
—ais
—ais
—ait
—ions
—iez
—aient

EXAMPLE:
PRESENT   nous donnons   nous finissons
           nous vendons
IMPERFECT   je donnais   je finissais
             je vendais

34

Here is the imperfect tense written out in full for each type of verb:

```
┌─ donner – to give ─┐    ┌─ dormir – to sleep ─┐
     je donnais              je dormais
     tu donnais              tu dormais
     il donnait              il dormait
     nous donnions           nous dormions
     vous donniez            vous dormiez
     ils donnaient           ils dormaient

┌─ vendre – to sell ─┐    ┌─ finir – to finish ─┐
     je vendais              je finissais
     tu vendais              tu finissais
     il vendait              il finissait
     nous vendions           nous finissions
     vous vendiez            vous finissiez
     ils vendaient           ils finissaient
```

The only exception to this rule is the verb 'être' (to be) where the imperfect is as follows:
j'étais
tu étais
il était
nous étions
vous étiez
ils étaient

Meaning and use of the imperfect tense

- The most important use of the imperfect tense is for descriptions in the past. These can be divided into:

  a Descriptions of people
  EXAMPLE:
  Elle avait les yeux bleus.
  She had blue eyes.

  Il portait un pullover noir.
  He was wearing a black jumper.

  b Descriptions of weather and scenery
  EXAMPLE:
  Il faisait chaud.
  It was hot.

  Les montagnes étaient couvertes de neige.
  The mountains were covered in snow.

  La route était déserte.
  The road was deserted.

  c Descriptions of feelings
  EXAMPLE:
  Marie était triste.
  Marie was sad.

  Maman était fâchée.
  Mum was angry.

  Les enfants étaient contents.
  The children were happy.

  Michel avait peur du chien.
  Michel was afraid of the dog.

- The imperfect tense is also used for repeated actions in the past, for instance, to translate 'used to' or when the words 'often' or 'every day', 'every morning' etc. appear.
  EXAMPLE:
  Elle se levait tous les jours à huit heures.
  She got up every day at eight o'clock.

  Chaque soir il allait au même bar.
  Every evening he used to go to the same bar.

  Mon oncle buvait toujours de la bière.
  My uncle always drank beer.

- The imperfect tense is also used to describe an action that was going on when something else occurred.
  In this sense it always translates into English as 'was —ing'.
  EXAMPLE:
  J'allais à l'école quand j'ai vu ta soeur.
  I was going to school when I saw your sister.

  Il lisait le journal quand je suis arrivé.
  He was reading the newspaper when I arrived.

- When changing direct speech to indirect speech, the present tense changes to the imperfect tense.
  EXAMPLE:
  Il a dit, ‹Je vais acheter un journal.›
  becomes
  Il a dit qu'il allait acheter un journal.

  Elle a dit, ‹Je me couche toujours à onze heures.›
  becomes
  Elle a dit qu'elle se couchait toujours à onze heures.

Note also that the pronoun has to change, as in the examples above, from 'je' to 'il' and from 'je' to 'elle'.
For more about changing direct to indirect speech, see the GRAMMAR SUMMARY in Dossier 10.

Negatives

Here is a list of negatives in French:
ne . . . pas
ne . . . point
ne . . . jamais – never
ne . . . plus – no longer, no more
ne . . . rien – nothing
ne . . . personne – nobody, no one
ne . . . que – only
ne . . . guère – scarcely
ne . . . ni . . . ni . . . – neither, nor

Position

- Generally speaking, the two parts of the negative go either side of the verb.
  EXAMPLE:
  Je ne vois pas.
  Il ne sort jamais.

- Note that where there is a pronoun object, 'ne' goes in front of the pronoun.
  EXAMPLE:
  Je ne le vois pas.

- Note that in the perfect or pluperfect tense, the negative generally goes either side of the auxiliary.
  EXAMPLE:
  Elle n'est pas sortie.
  Je n'ai rien vu.
  BUT:
  Je n'ai vu personne.

- With ne . . . que, 'que' comes immediately before the word to which it refers.
  EXAMPLE:
  Je ne suis allé à Paris que deux fois.
  I have been to Paris only twice.

- With ne . . . ni . . . ni, note that there is no article after 'ni'.
  EXAMPLE:
  Je n'ai ni frères ni soeurs.
  I have neither brothers nor sisters.

- Both parts of the negative come **before** an infinitive.
  EXAMPLE:
  Je t'ai dit de ne pas sortir.
  I told you not to go out.

  Il a décidé de ne rien faire.
  He decided not to do anything.

- The two parts of the negative are reversed where the negative would come first in English, i.e. where it is the subject of the sentence.
  EXAMPLE:
  Personne n'est entré.
  Nobody came in.

  Rien n'est prêt.
  Nothing is ready.

- **Sans** has a negative force like 'ne'.
  EXAMPLE:
  sans rien dire
  without saying anything

  sans rencontrer personne
  without meeting anybody

IMPORTANT

After a negative, 'du', 'de la', 'de l'' and 'des' become 'de'.
EXAMPLE:
J'ai du pain mais je n'ai pas de beurre.

This rule also applies to 'un' and 'une', except when meaning 'one'.
EXAMPLE:
J'ai un cahier mais je n'ai pas de stylo.

'Qui' and 'que'

These words are known as **relative pronouns** because they refer back to someone or something just previously mentioned.
- Use 'qui' as the subject of a verb.
- Use 'que' (or 'qu' before a vowel or silent 'h') as the direct object of a verb.
  EXAMPLE:
  Mon ami Paul, qui a dix-sept ans, travaille chez Renault.
  My friend Paul, who is seventeen, works at Renault's.

  L'appartement que nous avons loué est au troisième étage.
  The flat which we have rented is on the third floor.

Note that in the second example you could quite well leave out the word 'which' in English, but you CANNOT leave out the word 'que' in French.

DOSSIER 3
AU COLLEGE

READING COMPREHENSION

1

RENTRÉE SCOLAIRE

Annonce de la gare routière de Narbonne.
Cette annonce s'adresse aux élèves de Lézignan, inscrits en demi-pension dans les écoles de Narbonne et de Carcassonne. Les élèves désirant prendre quotidiennement les autobus de la ligne Narbonne – Carcassonne sont priés de venir retirer à la gare routière de Narbonne une carte d'abonnement provisoire contre la somme de cinquante francs. Ils devront ensuite fournir deux photos récentes et la fiche rose, signée par le directeur de leur collège. Ils recevront par la suite une carte d'abonnement permanente valable pour l'année scolaire entière.

a To whom is this announcement addressed? (Give as much detail as possible.)
b How much must pupils pay for a temporary season ticket?
c As well as two photographs, what must they then bring?
d For how long is a permanent season ticket valid?

2

Poitiers, le 7 février

Chère Debra

Merci pour ta gentille lettre. Je suis bien contente d'avoir une correspondante anglaise.

J'ai quatorze ans, et je vais à un collège mixte. Je suis en troisième. Cette année j'étudie neuf matières, les maths, le français, l'anglais, l'allemand, l'histoire, la géographie, la biologie, la chimie, et les travaux manuels. Aussi, je fais du sport le mercredi après-midi; du volley en hiver, du tennis en été.

Tu me dis dans ta lettre que tes cours ne durent que quarante minutes seulement. Tu as de la chance! Nos cours durent une heure. Et tu n'as qu'une heure de devoirs le soir. Moi, j'en ai deux. Mais en été j'ai dix semaines de vacances, et toi, tu n'en as que six, n'est-ce pas?

Ma soeur, Francine, qui a dix ans va à l'école primaire. Elle n'a qu'une demi-heure de devoirs chaque soir. Mon petit frère Marc, qui a quatre ans, va à la maternelle. Lui, bien sûr, il n'a pas de devoirs!

Comment est ton collège? Est-ce que c'est un collège mixte? Est-ce que tu dois porter l'uniforme scolaire? Est-ce que tu y vas à pied ou en autobus? Quelle est ta matière préférée?

Ecris-moi bientôt

Julie

VRAI OU FAUX?

When you have read Julie's letter, read carefully the following statements about it. Write 'vrai' for those which are correct. Rewrite those that are 'faux' so that they are correct.

a Julie est en troisième.
b Elle étudie la physique.
c Elle joue au volley le mercredi après-midi.
d Ses cours durent cinquante minutes.
e Les cours de Julie sont moins longs que les cours de Debra.
f Debra a plus de devoirs que Julie.
g Les vacances en France son moins longues que les vacances en Angleterre.
h Francine va à l'école primaire.
i Francine est plus âgée que Julie
j Marc est plus âgé que Francine.

Now answer in French the following questions:
a Quel âge a Julie?
b Combien de matières étudie-t-elle?
c Est-ce qu'elle fait du sport le jeudi?
d Qu'est-ce qu'elle fait comme sport en hiver?
e Est-ce que Julie a six semaines de vacances en été?
f Qui est Francine?
g Quel âge a-t-elle?
h Comment s'appelle le frère de Julie?

3
Two different points of view

Une élève parle

J'ai dix-sept ans. Je suis interne dans un lycée à Tours, et je ne m'y plais pas du tout. On n'a pas le droit de sortir de l'établissement, et il n'y a même pas un téléphone public pour neuf cents internes.

Le soir, l'étude est surveillée par des pions. On ne peut pas discuter avec les copains, on nous traite comme des gosses de dix ans.

Les professeurs ne s'intéressent absolument pas à nous. Ils veulent nous faire croire qu'il n'y a rien en dehors du travail. Pendant les cours on n'a le droit ni de discuter ni de poser des questions.

Moi, au fond, j'aime bien étudier. Mais vraiment, je commence à me révolter contre ce système inhumain.

Un professeur parle

En général, en France, il y a peu de rapports entre le professeur et ses élèves. Le professeur fait son cours, et puis il part. Il connaît très peu ses élèves, il leur parle à peine.

Depuis quelques années on essaie de changer ça, mais c'est très difficile. Les élèves ont tellement l'habitude de professeurs qui sont sévères, distants avec eux, que si un professeur essaie d'être sympathique et de discuter avec ses élèves ils en profitent et ils ne le respectent plus.

EITHER:
Translate the passages into English.
OR:
Answer in English the following questions:

Elève
a What sort of school does the student attend?
b Is he a day student or a boarder?
c What **two** general complaints does he make?
d What complaint does he make about evening study? Give as much detail as possible
e What **two** things can students not do in class?
f Why is he beginning to rebel against the system?

Professeur
g What, generally speaking, is the relationship between teacher and students in France?
h For how long have attempts been made to change the situation?
i What has been the students' reaction to these attempts?

4

The following passage is taken from the novel *Le Grand Meaulnes* by Alain-Fournier. In the first part of the book the author gives a clear picture of life at a small French country school at the beginning of the twentieth century.

◀ A une heure de l'après-midi, le lendemain, la salle de classe est claire, au milieu du paysage gelé, comme une barque sur l'Océan.

On a distribué les cahiers. Et, pendant que Monsieur Seurel écrit des problèmes au tableau, un silence imparfait s'établit, mêlé de conversations à voix basse, coupé de petits cris étouffés.

Monsieur Seurel, en copiant ses problèmes, pense à autre chose. Il se retourne de temps à autre, en regardant tout le monde d'un air à la fois sévère, et absent. Et ce remue-ménage cesse complètement, une seconde, pour reprendre ensuite, tout doucement d'abord.

Seul, au milieu de cette agitation, je me tais. Assis au bout d'une des tables de la division des plus jeunes, près des grandes fenêtres, je n'ai qu'à me redresser un peu pour apercevoir le jardin, le ruisseau en bas, puis les champs. ▶

EITHER:
Translate the passage into English.
OR:
Answer in English the following questions:
a During which season of the year did this scene occur? How do you know this?
b What **two** sounds broke the silence?
c What **two** facts are you told about the way Monsieur Seurel looked at the class?
d What happened when he looked round at the class?
e How do you know that the writer was one of the younger pupils?
f Where was he sitting?
g Name **three** things that he could see.

Answer in French the following questions:
a A quelle heure se passe cette scène?
b Que fait Monsieur Seurel?
c Que font les élèves?
d Que fait l'auteur?
e Qu'est-ce qu'il voit par la fenêtre?

LISTENING COMPREHENSION

1

You are going to hear two French teenagers talking about their school life. Listen carefully before answering in English the following questions:

Philippe

a How old is Philippe?
b What year is he in at school?
c At what time do lessons begin and end?
d Which is his favourite day, and why?
e Which is his best subject?
f What was his last mark for English?
g Philippe says he is a 'demi-pensionnaire'. What does this mean?
h What did he eat for main course for lunch today?

Yvette

a How old is Yvette? What relation is she to Philippe?
b What year is she in at school?
c When does she have lessons and Philippe does not?
d How many boarders (internes) are there at the lycée?
e What languages is she learning?
f Why has Yvette a lot of work?
g What do the pupils do during 'étude'?
h At what times do they have 'étude'?
i How often can they watch television?
j At what time do they go to bed?

2

It is the first day of the autumn term in a CES in Lille. Two pupils, Michelle and Janine, are talking during morning break. Listen carefully before answering in English the following questions:

a From which part of France does Janine come?
b Why has her family moved to Lille?
c In what type of place is Janine living at present?
d Where does Michelle live?
e What does Janine say about the school?
f Why is she afraid the pupils will laugh at her?
g What time is lunch?
h How often do they have ravioli?
i What does Janine say she has not yet been given?
j What is the first lesson in the afternoon?
k Why does Michelle like the English teacher?
l State **two** things you are told about Monsieur Boisvert.
m What is the next lesson?
n What happens if you arrive late for Monsieur Dassin's class?

GRAMMAR EXERCISES

1

You have learned that there are two ways of asking a question in French:
EITHER:
   By inverting the subject and verb.
OR:
   By using 'est-ce que'.

Translate these questions into French. Do five by inverting subject and verb, and five by using 'est-ce que'.
a Is she in the kitchen?
b Have Alain and Denise gone to the disco?
c Do you want to go to the youth club this evening?
d Why are your books on the table?
e Where is she?
f Have you telephoned the doctor?
g How much did you pay for the dinner?
h How are you?
i Will he come tomorrow?
j Is Madame Lebrun's son ill?

Copy the following passage. For each infinitive in brackets put the correct form of the verb. You will need to use either the present tense, the imperfect tense, or the imperative.

Je (s'appeler) Chantal. J'(avoir) douze ans. Je (aller) au CES Jéhan Ango à Dieppe, et je (être) en sixième. J'(aimer) bien l'anglais, c'(être) ma matière préférée. Le professeur d'anglais (être) très gentil. Quelquefois, il (dire) à un élève: «(Venir) au tableau noir! (Dessiner) une maison!» Mais le vendredi il (dire) toujours à la classe: «(Prendre) vos cahiers! (Ecrire) ces mots!» Je n'(aimer) pas ça! Je (faire) toujours des fautes! Si on (recevoir) une mauvaise note on (devoir) refaire l'exercice pendant l'heure du déjeuner.
Quand j'(être) à l'école primaire on (apprendre) un peu d'anglais. L'institutrice (être) gentille, elle (s'appeler) Madame Barthe. J'(aimer) bien l'école primaire. L'après-midi, on (faire) de la musique ou on (dessiner), et pour les leçons de géographie on (regarder) la télévision.

TRAVAIL ORAL

1

Read out the following, filling in the gaps.

Bonjour. Je m'appelle ——. J'ai —— ans. J'ai les cheveux —— et les yeux ——. Mon école s'appelle ——. Comme matières, je fais des mathématiques, de l'anglais, ——, ——, ——, ——, et ——. Ma matière préférée est ——. Le soir, je fais mes devoirs et puis je ——. Le weekend j'aime ——.

2

This exercise can best be done in pairs. Take it in turns to play each part.
Imagine that you are a French boy or girl, and that a new student has just arrived in your class. Ask him/her questions in French to obtain the following information: name; age; date of birthday; where he/she lives; whether he/she has any brothers or sisters; favourite subject; whether he/she likes sport, if so which sport(s); whether he/she likes music; what he/she does in the evenings and on Saturdays.
Then try to think of at least two more questions of your own.

3

You are Jean-Pierre, who is not a very well-organised boy in the mornings. Here is a conversation between Jean-Pierre and his mother. Ask all Jean-Pierre's questions in French.

(Ask your mum where your blue shirt is.)

Dans l'armoire.

(Ask her where your socks are.)

Dans le premier tiroir, à gauche.

(Ask if she has seen your English exercise book.)

Mais oui, il est sur la table.

(Ask what time it is.)

Il est huit heures moins dix.

(Ask her if it's raining.)

Non, mais il fait très froid.

(Ask if she has seen your anorak.)

Mais oui, il est ici, dans la cuisine. Dis, Jean-Pierre, tu rentres à quelle heure cet après-midi?

(Say you don't know. Why is she asking?)

Parce que je vais à l'hôpital cet après-midi, voir cette pauvre Madame Dupont. Alors, prends ta clef.

(Ask her where your key is.)

Je ne sais pas. Tu peux la chercher toi-même!

TRAVAIL ECRIT

1
Write the answers to the exercises in the TRAVAIL ORAL section.

2
Write a letter to your French penfriend describing your school as fully as possible. Ask him/her a few questions about his/her school. (*120 words.*)

3
Write a story which the following pictures suggest to you. Remember to use past tenses. (*120 words.*)

VOCABULARY

Reading comprehension

1
annonce (f) – (here) announcement
carte (f) d'abonnement – season ticket
fiche (f) – form, slip
fournir – to provide
gare (f) routière – bus/coach station
inscrit – enrolled
quotidiennement – daily
retirer – to collect
somme (f) – sum, amount
valable – valid

2
allemand – German
chimie (f) – chemistry
correspondant(e) – pen friend (m or f)
durer – to last
maternelle (f) – nursery school
travaux manuels (m pl) – craft

3
dehors – outside
depuis – for, since
essayer – to try
s'intéresser (à) – to be interested (in)
à peine – scarcely
pion (m) – supervisor
se plaire – to be pleased, happy
profiter – to take advantage
rapports (m pl) – relationship (between people)
se révolter – to rebel
surveillé – supervised
sympathique – friendly, pleasant
traiter – to treat
vraiment – really

4
absent – (here) absent-minded
d'abord – at first
apercevoir – to perceive, to see
autre – other
barque (f) – boat
au bout de – at the end of
champ (m) – field
clair – light
étouffé – stifled, suppressed
gelé – frozen
imparfait – imperfect
lendemain (m) – next day
au milieu de – in the middle of
paysage (m) – landscape, countryside
ruisseau (m) – stream, small river
se redresser – to sit up straight
remue-ménage (m) – stir, bustle

Listening comprehension

1
aîné – elder
bac. (abbreviation of 'baccalauréat') – French school-leaving examination needed for entry to university and higher education.
cours (m) – lesson
dur – hard
espagnol – Spanish
étude (f) – study, study time
frites (f pl) – chips
interne (m or f) – boarder
langue (f) – language
loin – far
lycée (m) – upper school (ages 15 to 19)
matière (f) – subject
prochain – next
radis (m) – radish
rôti – roast
seulement – only
trop – too, too much, too many
yaourt (m) – yoghourt

2
chômage (m) – unemployment
cloche (f) – bell
se dépêcher – to hurry
élève (m or f) – pupil
emploi (m) du temps – timetable
envoyer – to send
(de) mauvaise humeur – (in) a bad mood
Midi (m) – the south of France
se moquer (de) – to make fun (of), to laugh (at)
oublier – to forget
prof. (abbreviation of 'professeur') – teacher
quelquefois – sometimes
repas (m) – meal
sonner – to ring
voyager – to travel

45

GRAMMAR

Asking questions

There are **two** basic ways of asking a question in French.
1 By putting 'est-ce que' in front of a statement.
   EXAMPLE:
   Tu connais Michel.   You know Michel.
   Est-ce que tu connais Michel?   Do you know Michel?

2 By inverting the subject and verb.
   EXAMPLE:
   Tu connais Michel.   You know Michel.
   Connais-tu Michel?   Do you know Michel?

Note
In talking, French people frequently ask a question simply by making a statement, but in a 'questioning' tone of voice.

EXAMPLE:
Tu viens?   Are you coming?
Il est là?   Is he there?

Questions in the perfect tense

EXAMPLE:
Avez-vous acheté des timbres?
Have you bought some stamps?

Est-elle partie hier?
Did she leave yesterday?

Vous êtes-vous couché de bonne heure?
Did you go to bed early?

You can, of course, use 'est-ce que' instead, and it is certainly simpler to do so with reflexive verbs.
EXAMPLE:
Est-ce que vous vous êtes couché de bonne heure?
Did you go to bed early?

When the subject of the question is not just a pronoun, here is the method to use:

Monsieur Dutan est-il dans le jardin?
Is Monsieur Dutan in the garden?

That is you state the subject, then repeat it as a pronoun in the question.
EXAMPLE:
Le garçon aux cheveux frisés, était-il à la maison des jeunes?
Was the boy with curly hair at the youth club?

Question words

These should be learnt by heart.

qui?	who?
que?	what?
quand?	when?
où?	Where?
pourquoi?	why?
combien (de)?	how much?/how many?
comment?	how?

EXAMPLE:
Qui est là?   Who is there?
Que faites-vous?   What are you doing?
Quand veux-tu voir le film?   When do you want to see the film?
Combien de cartes postales as-tu acheté?   How many cards did you buy?
Ça fait combien? } How much is it?
Ça coûte combien? }

BE CAREFUL when using 'comment?' Note the difference between:
Comment allez-vous? } How are you?
Comment vas-tu?   }
and
Comment est-il?   What is he like?

Other question forms

Quel disque as-tu acheté?   Which record did you buy?
Quelle heure est-il?   What time is it?
(quels = *m pl*   quelles = *f pl*)

46

Lequel de ces T-shirts préfères-tu?
Which one of these T-shirts do you prefer?

Laquelle de ces robes vas-tu acheter?
Which one of these dresses are you going to buy?
(lesquels = m pl   lesquelles = f pl)

The answers to the 'lequel', 'laquelle', 'lesquels', 'lesquelles', questions are:
celui-ci = this one   celui-là = that one
celle-ci   celle-là
ceux-ci = these ones   ceux-là = those ones
celles-ci   celles-là

Qu'est-ce qui? = What? (as subject)
EXAMPLE:
Qu'est-ce qui se passe?   What is going on?
Qu'est-ce qui est arrivé?   What has happened?

Qu'est-ce que? = What? (as object)
EXAMPLE:
Qu'est-ce qu'elle a fait?   What has she done?
Qu'est-ce que vous voulez dire?   What do you mean?

Comparisons

plus . . . que   more . . . than
moins . . . que   less . . . than
aussi . . . que   as . . . as

EXAMPLE:
Pierre est plus intelligent que Paul.
Pierre is more intelligent than Paul.

Mais il est moins intelligent que Philippe
But he is less intelligent than Philippe.

Je suis aussi intelligent que Philippe.
I am as intelligent as Philippe.

● **Note**
In French, there is no equivalent of adding —er to an adjective as in English (tall, taller). You must use '**plus**'.
EXAMPLE:
Il est plus grand que toi.
He is taller than you.
BUT:
The comparative of bon   good
             is meilleur   better.
EXAMPLE:
J'ai une bonne idée, allons au cinéma.
I've got a good idea, let's go to the cinema!

Moi, j'ai une meilleure idée, allons à la disco!
I've got a better idea, let's go to the disco!

DOSSIER 4
ON FAIT DES COURSES

READING COMPREHENSION

1

You might see all the following signs in a large French department store such as *Nouvelles Galeries, Dames de France*, etc.
Match each one with its correct meaning.

Signs:
- tirez
- bijouterie
- ameublement
- tapis
- CAISSE
- SORTIE
- parfumerie
- literie
- RAYON ENFANT
- poussez
- fourrures
- rayon disques

MEANING
cash desk
children's department
bedding
furs
record department
pull
furnishings
perfumes
carpets
push
jewellery
exit

2

You might see all the following signs during a shopping expedition in a French town.
Match up each sign with its correct meaning.

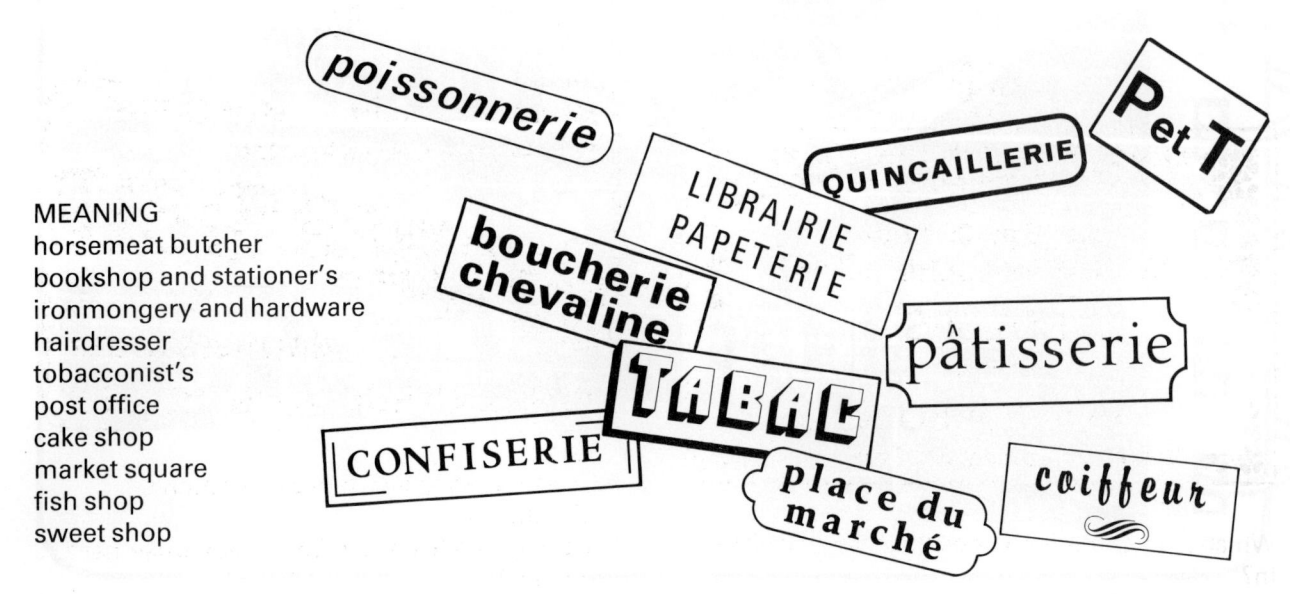

Signs:
- poissonnerie
- QUINCAILLERIE
- P et T
- LIBRAIRIE PAPETERIE
- boucherie chevaline
- pâtisserie
- TABAC
- CONFISERIE
- place du marché
- coiffeur

MEANING
horsemeat butcher
bookshop and stationer's
ironmongery and hardware
hairdresser
tobacconist's
post office
cake shop
market square
fish shop
sweet shop

50

3

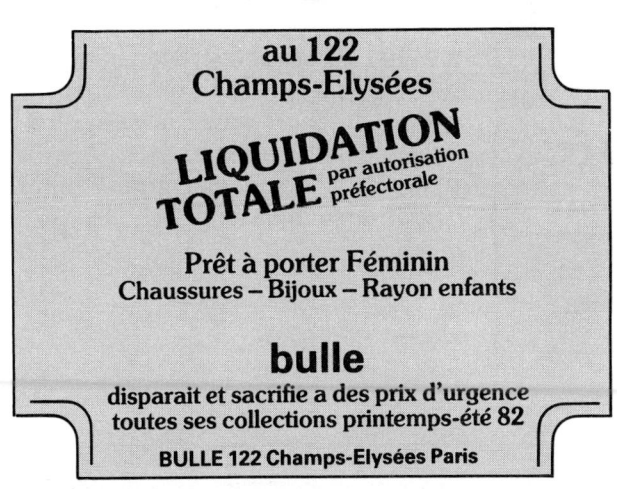

au 122 Champs-Elysées

LIQUIDATION TOTALE par autorisation préfectorale

Prêt à porter Féminin
Chaussures – Bijoux – Rayon enfants

bulle

disparait et sacrifie a des prix d'urgence
toutes ses collections printemps-été 82

BULLE 122 Champs-Elysées Paris

Name **three** things you can buy in this shop as well as women's clothes.

4

ÉLOIGNEZ LES INSECTES AVANT QU'ILS NE VOUS PIQUENT!

pick-out

CRÈME ET LOTION
en pharmacie

a What purpose do these products serve?
b In which sort of shop could you buy them?

5

du 25 au 29 Août
GRANDE BRADERIE sur les
SOLDES
à la
BOITE A PULL
8, rue des Marchands. Perpignan

Which item of clothing does this shop specialise in?

6

PIERRE DALREY

chemisier créateur
HOMME – FEMME
plusieurs longueurs de manches
POPELINE DE COTON

47, rue Pierre-Charron   Tél 225.01.12

a What type of clothing is sold here?
b What is special about the sizes in which these garments are made?

7

PLUS que JAMAIS...
la barbe
c'est l'affaire des spécialistes
TOUS LES RASOIRS
ELECTRIQUES OU
MECANIQUES
DIDIER-NEVEUR
39, rue MARBEUF – Tél: 225.81.70
Suc. 20, rue de la Paix, PARIS–6e - 2e

What is sold here?

8

pierre balmain   MONSIEUR

Dans la limite des stocks soldés

SOLDES D'ETE

3 derniers jours

6, GRAND'RUE - MONTPELLIER

a Does this shop sell men's or women's clothing?
b During which season did this advertisement appear?

51

DERNIERS JOURS   DERNIERS JOURS

AVANT FERMETURE ANNUELLE
LE COMPTOIR FRANCE ORIENT
**SOLDE 10.000 TAPIS D'ORIENT
à des PRIX JAMAIS VUS**

Tous les jours de 10H à 19H sauf le Dimanche - vendus avec
CERTIFICAT D'ORIGINE - CREDIT GRATUIT
15, RUE DIEU - 75010 PARIS - Tél.: 239.32.00
Métro République

9
a What is being advertised here?
b When exactly is this shop open?
c Why are there only a few days left in which to go there?
d Which is the nearest underground station to this shop?

10
a For whom does this shop cater?
b During which season is this advertisement being shown?
c What are you told about the prices?

AU CHAT BOTTÉ
tout pour l'enfant de 0 à 12 ans

SOLDES D'HIVER

tout à moitié prix
Dépêchez-vous! Trois jours seulement!

LOUIS GIRAUD
Avenue d'Espagne, Béziers
SOLDES
à partir du 1er août
Prix imbattables
EXEMPLES:
Robe (dames)   ~~200F~~   95F
Robe (enfants)   ~~150F~~   75F
Pantalon   ~~190F~~   110F
Chemise   ~~132F~~   84F
T-shirts, pulls
hommes, femmes, enfants, moitié prix

11
a When do these sales start?
b What are you told about the prices?
c By how much has a lady's dress been reduced?
d How much would a man save if he bought a pair of trousers and two shirts in the sale?
e What reduction is there on T-shirts and pullovers?

12
What do the following signs mean?

FERMETURE ANNUELLE
à partir du 1er août jusqu'au 2 septembre

HEURES D'OUVERTURE:
mardi, mercredi, jeudi; 9h. à 18h.30
vendredi, samedi; 9h. à 20.00
Fermé: dimanche, lundi

Fermé les jours fériés

13

AUBERGE DU LION D'OR

MENU à 35F
crudités ou charcuterie

côtelette de porc ou langue de boeuf
avec salade et pommes frites

glace ou fruit

MENU à 50F
salade de tomates
radis au beurre
melon

rôti de boeuf
escalope de veau
poulet froid
avec petits pois ou salade, frites

glace
crème caramel
fruit

MENU GASTRONOMIQUE à 85F
melon au porto
6 escargots farcis
6 huîtres

truite aux amandes
moules marinières
sole meunière

coq au vin
canard à l'orange (10F sup.)
boeuf bourguignon
légumes: petits pois, haricots verts,
pommes de terre rôties, frites, purée

fromage, salade de fruits, tarte maison
mousse au chocolat

SERVICE COMPRIS **VIN EN SUS
COUVERT 10F**

a If you like raw vegetables, which starter will you choose on the 35F menu?
b Which meat, in various forms, appears on all three menus?
c Which menu must you choose if you want veal?
d On which menu can you have a cold main course, and what is it?
e If you are having the 85F menu and you don't like snails or oysters, what must you choose?
f If you want a hot chicken dish as your main course, which menu must you choose?
g Name **two** fish you could have as a second course on the 85F menu.
h Which main dish on this menu is special, and why?
i What types of potato can you have on the 85F menu?
j If you want a home-made dessert, what must you choose?
k What are you told about wine?
l What additional charges will you have to pay?

14

The following passage is taken from *Poil de Carotte* by Jules Renard.

Poil de Carotte (carrot-head, i.e. he has red hair,) is an unhappy small boy. His mother is extremely strict, sometimes unkind, and he is very afraid of her, but, as you will see, he finally rebels.

MADAME LEPIC	Mon petit Poil de Carotte, chéri, je t'en prie, tu serais bien mignon d'aller me chercher une livre de beurre au moulin. Cours vite. On t'attendra pour se mettre à table.
POIL DE CAROTTE	Non, maman.
MADAME LEPIC	Pourquoi réponds-tu 'non maman'? Si, nous t'attendrons.
POIL DE CAROTTE	Non maman, je n'irai pas au moulin.
MADAME LEPIC	Comment! Tu n'iras pas au moulin? Que dis-tu? Est-ce que tu rêves?
POIL DE CAROTTE	Non maman.
MADAME LEPIC	Voyons, Poil de Carotte. Je t'ordonne d'aller tout de suite chercher une livre de beurre au moulin.
POIL DE CAROTTE	J'ai entendu. Je n'irai pas.
MADAME LEPIC	Comment! Que se passe-t-il? Pour la première fois de ta vie, tu refuses de m'obéir?
POIL DE CAROTTE	Oui maman.
MADAME LEPIC	Tu refuses d'obéir à ta mère.
POIL DE CAROTTE	A ma mère, oui maman.
MADAME LEPIC	Ça, par exemple! Fileras-tu?
POIL DE CAROTTE	Non maman.
MADAME LEPIC	Veux-tu te taire et filer?
POIL DE CAROTTE	Je me tairai, sans filer.

Poil de Carotte se tait, et ne bouge pas. C'est, en effet, la première fois que Poil de Carotte lui dit non. Si encore elle le dérangeait! S'il avait été en train de jouer! Mais, assis par terre, il se tournait les pouces, les yeux fermés. Et maintenant il la dévisage, tête haute. Les secondes passent.

‹C'est évidemment la fin du monde,› dit enfin Madame Lepic, ‹Je laisse donc ton père t'en parler.›

‹Papa›, dit Poil de Carotte, ‹si tu le veux, j'irai chercher cette livre de beurre au moulin, j'irai pour toi, pour toi seulement. Je refuse d'y aller pour ma mère.›

Monsieur Lepic semble plus ennuyé que flatté de cette préférence. Mal à l'aise, il fait quelques pas dans l'herbe, hausse les épaules, tourne le dos, et rentre à la maison.

Answer in English the following questions:
a What does Madame Lepic ask Poil de Carotte to do?
b What does she say they will not do until he returns?
c Why is Madame Lepic so surprised at her son's behaviour?
d What had he been doing when she made her request?
e What, according to Madame Lepic, must obviously be about to occur?
f On what condition does Poil de Carotte say he will do as asked?
g What is his father's reaction?
h Name **four** things his father then does.

Translate into English from 'Poil de Carotte se tait . . .' to the end of the passage.

Answer in French the following questions, using pronouns where possible:
a Est-ce que Poil de Carotte doit aller chercher du beurre à l'épicerie?
b Est-ce qu'on se mettra à table sans lui?
c Est-ce qu'il ira au moulin?
d Est-ce qu'il dit souvent ‹non› à sa mère?
e Est-ce qu'il refuse d'aller chercher la livre de beurre pour son père?
f Est-ce que Monsieur Lepic est flatté de la préférence de son fils?

LISTENING COMPREHENSION

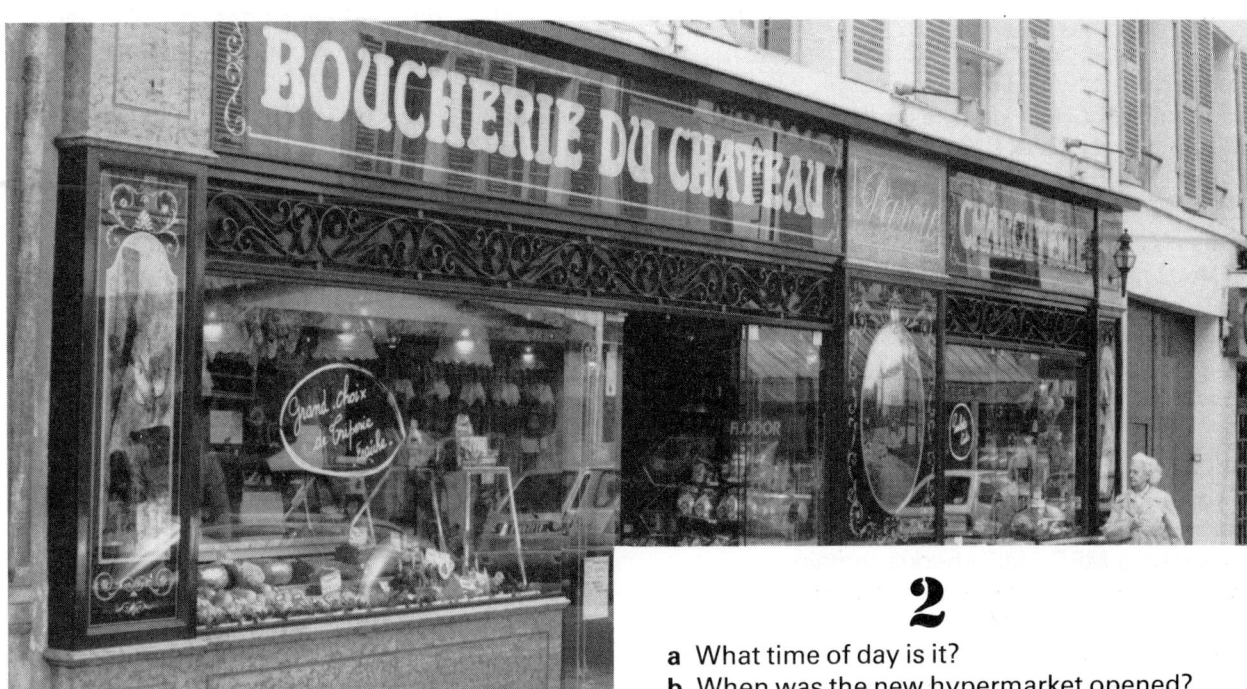

Listen carefully to the passage before answering in English the following questions:

1

a At what time did Madame Petit wake-up?
b Why did she take an aspirin?
c What was she going to take in which to carry her shopping?
d How long did she have to wait for the bus?
e Which shop did she visit first?
f What did she buy at the baker's shop?
g Where exactly did she find her purse?
h Why did she buy aspirins at the chemist's shop?
i What else did she buy there?
j Where did she meet Madame Renoir?
k How did the two ladies travel home?

2

a What time of day is it?
b When was the new hypermarket opened?
c How did Madame Lebon find out about it?
d What is being done to attract clients?
e Name **two** items on which Madame Lebon says prices are reduced.
f What does Lisette say about the price of records?
g Which other offer does Lisette mention that interests her?
h Which **two** items does Lisette say might interest her father?
i What will Monsieur Lebon do at about half past five tomorrow?

Le lendemain
j What time is it now, and where are they?
k What does Monsieur Lebon say about the wallpapers?
l What was wrong with the lawn mowers?
m What does Lisette say about the records?
n What does Lisette say about the jeans?
o Why, according to Madame Lebon, were the sheets not really cheap?
p What consolation does Lisette offer?
q What does Lisette suggest?
r What does Lisette say she will do?

55

GRAMMAR EXERCISES

1

Rewrite these sentences, replacing the words in capital letters with a **direct** object pronoun.
a Je vois LE CHIEN dans le jardin.
b Elle cherche SON CHEMISIER BLANC.
c Papa allume UNE PIPE.
d Nous achetons LES BONBONS.
e Ils n'écoutent pas LE PROFESSEUR.
f Vous ne voyez pas CHARLES.
g Tu as LES DISQUES.
h On cherche L'HOTEL.

2

Rewrite these sentences, replacing the words in capital letters with an **indirect** object pronoun.
a J'écris A MES AMIS chaque semaine.
b Il envoie un cadeau A SA SOEUR.
c Elle téléphone A FRANÇOISE.
d Tu dois répondre AU PROFESSEUR.
e Nous avons donné les cahiers AUX ELEVES.
f J'ai demandé dix francs A MA MERE.
g Nous donnons du lait AU CHAT.
h Elle permet AUX ENFANTS de jouer dans le jardin.

3

Write either: **du**; **de la**; **de l'**; **des**; **de**; **d'** at each number in the following conversation.

Bonjour, madame. Je voudrais un kilo (**1**) tomates, s'il vous plaît.
Oui, mademoiselle. Et avec ça?
Vous avez (**2**) pommes?
Non, je regrette, je n'ai pas (**3**) pommes, mais j'ai (**4**) bananes.
Bon, une livre (**5**) bananes. Vous avez (**6**) eau minérale?
Non, je n'ai pas (**7**) eau minérale, mais j'ai (**8**) limonade.
Eh bien, donnez-moi deux bouteilles (**9**) limonade et une bouteille (**10**) vin rouge. Et puis, j'ai besoin (**11**) sucre. Donnez-moi un paquet (**12**) sucre et un petit paquet (**13**) beurre.
C'est tout, mademoiselle?
Non. Je voudrais (**14**) confiture, un pot (**15**) confiture aux fraises. Et trois tranches (**16**) jambon.
Désolée, mademoiselle. Je n'ai plus (**17**) jambon, mais j'ai (**18**) pâté.
Alors, donnez-moi trois tranches (**19**) pâté, et cent grammes (**20**) olives. Voilà! C'est tout!

TRAVAIL ORAL

2 baguettes
200 grammes fromage
4 tranches jambon
bouteille vin rouge
bouteille eau minérale
paquet sucre
6 oeufs
boite sardines
livre café

1

Here is Madame Lenoir's shopping list. Practise asking for the items listed.

Try to use different beginnings for your sentences.
EXAMPLE:
Je voudrais . . .
Donnez-moi . . .
Avez-vous . . .

2

You are going for a picnic with three friends. Ask for suitable things at 'une alimentation' (general food shop). If you prefer, write out a shopping list in French beforehand.

3

You are camping in France with your family. Your mother sends you to buy food for Sunday lunch. You need meat, two vegetables, something for dessert, some fruit, and a bottle of wine. Make a list in French, and then practise asking for the things you want.

4

Work in pairs. One of you is the customer, and must ask for at least four items. The other is the shopkeeper, who does not have any of the things requested, but always suggests an alternative.
EXAMPLE:
Vous avez du Coca-Cola?
Non, je regrette, je n'ai pas de Coca-Cola, mais j'ai de la bière.

5

Practise the following scene in pairs. You should both practise both parts.
You are on holiday in France, and you have gone to *Nouvelles Galeries* to buy a T-shirt.

(Ask where you can find T-shirts.)

Les T-shirts? C'est le rayon sportif. Au premier étage à gauche.

(Thank her.)

You go to the first floor.

(Say you would like a white T-shirt, size 40.)

Bien, mademoiselle. Nous avons celui-ci, qui est très joli.

(Ask if you can try it on.)

Bien sûr, mademoiselle.

(Say it's too big.)

Eh bien, essayez la taille 38.

(Say yes, it's fine. Ask how much it is.)

C'est soixante-quinze francs, mademoiselle.

(Say it's too dear. Ask if she has any cheaper T-shirts.)

Oui mademoiselle. Nous avons ces T-shirts à 40 francs.

(Say that's very cheap. You'll take three – in white, red, and black.)

Merci, mademoiselle. Passez à la caisse, s'il vous plaît.

6

Refer to the menu in the READING COMPREHENSION section and order a meal for yourself and a friend.

TRAVAIL ECRIT

1

Write to your French penfriend, telling him/her about a recent shopping expedition when you spent the money which you had received for your birthday.

2

Write a story in French, using past tenses, based on the following outline:
Le dernier jour de vacances en France – vous allez en ville acheter des cadeaux – vous laissez votre porte-monnaie (ou votre portefeuille) dans un magasin – vos efforts pour le retrouver – la journée finit bien.

3

Write a story, in past tenses, which the following pictures suggest to you.

VOCABULARY

Reading comprehension

1
ameublement (*m*) – furniture, furnishings
bijouterie (*f*) – jewellery
caisse (*f*) – cash desk
fourrure (*f*) – fur
literie (*f*) – bedding
parfumerie (*f*) – shop, department, selling perfume
pousser – to push
rayon (*m*) – department (in a large shop)
tapis (*f*) – carpet
tirer – to pull

2
boucherie (*f*) chevaline – horse-butcher's shop
coiffeur (*m*) – hairdresser
confiserie (*f*) – sweet shop
librairie (*f*) – bookshop
marché (*m*) – market
papeterie (*f*) – stationer's shop
pâtisserie – cake shop
P et T – post office
place (*f*) – square
poissonnerie (*f*) – fish shop

3

4
éloigner – to chase, send away
piquer – to bite, sting (insects)

6
chemisier (*m*) – shirt
manche (*f*) – sleeve
plusieurs – several

7
barbe (*f*) – beard
rasoir (*m*) – razor

9
fermeture (*f*) – closure
sauf – except
tapis (*m*) – carpet, rug

10
moitié (*f*) – half
prix (*m*) – price
soldes (*m pl*) – sales

11
à partir de – from (with dates, times)
chemise (*f*) – shirt
imbattable – unbeatable
pantalon (*m*) – trousers

12
jour (*m*) férié – public holiday
jusqu'à – until
ouverture (*f*) – opening

13
canard (*m*) – duck
charcuterie (*f*) – cooked meat (ham, etc.)
coq (*m*) au vin – chicken in wine sauce
crudités (*f pl*) – raw vegetable salad
escalope (*f*) – cutlet (usually veal)
escargot (*m*) – snail
fromage (*m*) – cheese
haricots (*m pl*) verts – green beans
huître (*f*) – oyster
langue (*f*) – tongue
légume (*m*) – vegetable
moule (*f*) – mussel
petits pois (*m pl*) – peas
(pommes) frites – chips
purée – mash
radis (*m*) – radish
rôti – roast
truite (*f*) – trout
veau (*m*) – veal

14
bouger – to move
déranger – to disturb, interrupt
dévisager – to stare
dos (*m*) – back
ennuyé – embarassed
filer – to go, run along
fin (*f*) – end
flatté – flattered
fois (*f*) – time
(la première fois – the first time)
hausser les épaules – to shrug one's shoulders
herbe (*f*) – grass
livre (*f*) – pound (weight or money)
mal à l'aise – ill at ease
monde (*m*) – world
moulin (*m*) – mill
obéir – to obey
pas (*m*) – step
pouce (*m*) – thumb
rêver – to dream
sembler – to seem
se passer – to happen
se taire – to be silent
terre (*f*) – ground, earth
tout de suite – at once
vite – quickly

Listening comprehension

1
attendre – to wait
baguette (*f*) – long French loaf
bavarder – to chat
boeuf (*m*) – beef
boucher (*m*) – butcher
boulangerie (*f*) – baker's shop
comptoir (*m*) – counter
croissant (*m*) – crescent-shaped roll
laisser – to leave
panier (*m*) – basket
pharmacie (*f*) – chemist's shop
rencontrer – to meet

2
années (*f pl*) soixante-dix – the seventies
apéritif (*m*) – drink before a meal
attirer – to attract
batterie (*f*) de cuisine – kitchen utensils

59

bricolage (m) – do-it-yourself
casserole (f) – saucepan
client (m) – customer
couverture (f) – blanket
drap (m) – sheet
économiser – to save money
en prime – as a free gift
folie (f) – (here) nonsense, rubbish
intéressant – (here) good, reasonable
journal (m) – newspaper
marque (f) – make
meilleur marché - cheaper
moitié (f) – half
ouverture (f) – opening
papier (m) peint – wallpaper
paraître – to seem
prix (m) – price
propriété (f) – large house, estate
taille (f) – size
tas (m) – (here) a lot (slang)
tondeuse (f) – lawn mower
tube (m) – hit record

GRAMMAR

Du, de la, de l', des

The English word 'some' is translated in French by 'du', 'de la', 'de l'', or 'des'.
EXAMPLE:
J'ai acheté du pain.
Elle a pris de la confiture.
Veux-tu de l'eau minérale?
Nous avons acheté des pommes et des bananes.

● Note that the word 'some' can sometimes be left out in English, but, in French, you cannot leave out 'du', 'de la', 'de l'' or 'des'.
EXAMPLE:
She bought bread, cheese, and lemonade.
Elle a acheté du pain, du fromage, et de la limonade.

There are **two** types of sentence where you must use 'de' or 'd'' instead of 'du', 'de la', 'de l'' or 'des':

1 After a negative.
 EXAMPLE:
 Vous avez du pain? Non, je n'ai pas de pain.
 Vous avez de la limonade? Non, je n'ai pas de limonade.
 Vous avez de l'eau minérale? Non, je n'ai pas d'eau minérale.
 Vous avez des croissants? Non, je n'ai pas de croissants.

2 If a quantity of the item is stated. (For this purpose 'a glass of . . . ', 'a cup of . . . ', 'a box of . . . ' counts as quantity.)
 EXAMPLE:
 Je voudrais un paquet de sucre.
 Donnez-moi une livre de fraises et un kilo de tomates.
 Avez-vous une boîte d'allumettes?
 Voulez-vous une tasse de thé?
 Voulez-vous un peu de fromage?

Direct object pronouns

EXAMPLE:
Je vois Paul tous les jours.   Je **le** vois tous les jours.
I see Paul every day.   I see him every day.

Il vend la voiture.   Il **la** vend.
He is selling the car.   He is selling it.

Je vois mes amis tous les soirs.   Je **les** vois tous les soirs.
I see my friends every evening.   I see them every evening

The words in **heavy type** are direct object pronouns, i.e. they replace the nouns which are the object of the verb.
le replaces 'Paul'
la replaces 'la voiture'
les replaces 'mes amis'

Here is a complete list of direct object pronouns:

```
me = me (change to m' before a vowel)
te = you (change to t' before a vowel)
le = him/it (m) (change to l' before a vowel)
la = her/it (f) (change to l' before a vowel)
nous = us
vous = you
les = them (m and f)
```

You will have noticed from the first examples given that the French word order is different from the English. In French, the direct object pronoun precedes the verb.
EXAMPLE:
Tu as ton parapluie? Oui, je l'ai.
Have you got your umbrella? Yes, I have got it.

Est-ce qu'il regarde la télévision? Oui, il la regarde.
Is he watching television? Yes he is watching it.

● There is one important exception to this rule. With the imperative, i.e. when giving orders or instructions, the direct object pronoun **follows** the verb, and is linked to it by a hyphen.
EXAMPLE :
Prends les assiettes et donne-les à ta mère.
Take the plates and give them to your mother.

Le professeur parle, écoutez-le.
The teacher is talking, listen to him.
BUT:
If the order is a negative one (don't do something) you go back to the normal word order:
EXAMPLE:
Ne les donne pas.
Don't give them.

Ne l'écoutez pas.
Don't listen to him.

Indirect object pronouns

EXAMPLE:
Je parle à Françoise.   Je **lui** parle.
I am talking to Françoise.   I am talking to her.

Elle donne des cadeaux   Elle **leur** donne des
  à ses amis.   cadeaux.
She gives presents   She gives presents to them.
  to her friends.   She gives them presents.

The words in **heavy type** are indirect object pronouns.
lui replaces 'à Françoise'.
leur replaces 'à ses amis'.

Here is a complete list of indirect object pronouns:

```
me = to me
te = to you
lui = to him/her
nous = to us
vous = to you
leur = to them (m and f)
```

● Note that these pronouns, just like direct object pronouns, precede the verb. Also, there is the same exception in the case of the imperative.
EXAMPLE:
Prête-lui ton stylo.
Lend him your pen.
BUT:
Ne lui prête pas ton stylo.
Don't lend him your pen.

● Note that after the imperative 'me' and 'te' become 'moi' and 'toi'.
EXAMPLE :
Donne-moi le livre.
Give me the book.
BUT:
Ne me donne pas le livre.
Don't give me the book.

When there is more than one object pronoun in a sentence, the order of pronouns is as follows:

me		
te	le	lui
se	la	leur
nous	les	
vous		

EXAMPLE:
Il me la donne.
He gives it to me.

Elle nous les rend.
She gives them back to us.

Je le leur apporte.
I bring it to them.

The pronouns 'en' and 'y'

en = some, any, of it, of them
EXAMPLE:
Tu as des crayons? Oui, j'en ai deux.
Have you any pencils? Yes, I have two (of them).

Avez-vous des disques? Oui, nous en avons beaucoup.
Have you any records? Yes, we have a lot (of them).

y = there, to it (place)
EXAMPLE:
Tu vas au cinéma? Oui, j'y vais.
Are you going to the cinema? Yes, I'm going there.

Tu connais Paris? Oui, j'y suis allé l'année dernière.
Do you know Paris? Yes, I went there last year.

Pronoun order

'En' and 'y' follow the direct and indirect pronouns in a sentence, but, like them, they precede the verb (except in the imperative).
'Y' precedes 'en' when they both occur in the same sentence.

EXAMPLE:
Tu donnes des bonbons à ton frère? Oui, je lui en donne. Alors, donne-m'en aussi.
Are you giving some sweets to your brother? Yes, I am giving him some. Well then give me some too.

Est-ce qu'il y a des fleurs dans le jardin? Oui, il y en a beaucoup.
Are there some flowers in the garden? Yes, there are a lot (of them).

● Note the following types of sentences with 'en' and 'y':
J'ai besoin de ce stylo.   I need this pen.
BECOMES:
J'en ai besoin.   I need it. (i.e. I have need of it.)

Tu te souviens de ce film? Oui je m'en souviens.
Do you remember that film? Yes, I remember it.
BUT:
Tu te souviens de Louise? Oui, je me souviens d'elle.
Do you remember Louise? Yes I remember her.

J'espère que tu penses à ton travail de temps en temps. J'y pense souvent.
I hope you think about your work now and then. I often think about it.
BUT:
Est-ce que tu penses à ton père? Oui, je pense à lui.
Are you thinking about your father? Yes, I'm thinking about him.

DOSSIER 5

SPORT ET LOISIRS

READING COMPREHENSION

1

ASSAUT DE LA MANCHE

Seize nageurs, dont une équipe de six handicapés, ont entrepris, hier matin, la traversée de la Manche en partant de Douvres.

Parmi ces nageurs se trouve un instituteur britannique, âgé de soixante-cinq ans. S'il réussit, il deviendra l'homme le plus âgé à avoir traversé la Manche à la nage.

L'équipe de six nageurs handicapés de nationalité française veut tenter une double traversée.

a How many swimmers are involved?
b What exactly did they try to do and when?
c What is the job of the British man?
d How old is he?
e If he succeeds, in what way will it be a 'first'?
f What are the six handicapped people attempting?

2

Le motocycliste, Johann Klein, a été interdit de toute compétition étrangère par sa fédération pour avoir quitté le podium, dimanche à Nurburg pendant l'exécution de l'hymne national pour protester contre le chômage dans son pays.

Johann a dit: ‹Mes amis et de nombreux mécaniciens sont au chômage, et le gouvernement ne fait rien contre cet état de choses.›

Monsieur Kurt Busch, président de la fédération du motocyclisme ouest-allemande a répondu: ‹Nous ne pouvons tolérer qu'un tel sportif nous représente à l'étranger. Cela porterait un coup à la réputation de l'Allemagne fédérale.›

a What nationality is Johann Klein?
b What has he been forbidden to do?
c When did he leave the platform on Sunday?
d What was he protesting about?
e Which **two** groups of people did he say had been affected?
f Why, according to Kurt Busch, has Johann been banned?

3

TF1 — JEUDI 15 AVRIL

12.05 Le temps vivre, le temps d'almer

Feuilleton. Scénario et adaptation : Louis GROSPIERRE, Raymond ASSAYAS et Alain QUERCY. Réalisation : Louis GROSPIERRE. (9e épisode).
Installée dans ses nouvelles fonctions, Mathilde tente de réorganiser l'usine. Elle aménage aussi sa nouvelle résidence, la maison de l'ancien directeur...

12.30 Les visiteurs du jour

13.00 TF 1 Actualités

13.35 Télévision régional

13.50 Objectif santé

« L'aide aux vacances des classes d'Allocations familiaies »

16.30 Dessin animé

Maya l'Abeille : « Alexandre imprésario »

16.55 Croque-Vacances

Emission de Claude PIERRARD. Réalisation : Gérard BOULOUYS.
■ 16.55 Desain animé. Sans Secret : « Sans secret est en vacances ».
■ Première partie du bricoiage par Joele FARNA, « L'arbre à oeufs ».
■ Variétés. Gérard LENORMAND chante « La Petite valse » et « Chanson d'innocence ».
■ Isidore et Clémentine.
■ Infos-Magazine « Vacances à la ferme ». Foyer familial « La Marelle » (Vosges).
■ Dessin animé. Woody Woodpecker : « Employé municipal ».
■ Cirque. Les artistes du cirque de Paris présentent un numéro de chiens dressés.
■ Seconde partie du bricolage : « L'arbre à œufs ».
■ Feuilleton. « Mon ami Ben ». « Le Dernier loup rouge ».

18.00 C'est à vous

18.25 Un, rue Sésame

« L'Invitation à déjeuner »

18.45 Quotidiennement vôtre

Jean-Paul SARTRE : Deux ans déjà.

18.50 Les paris de TF 1

Avec Paul PRÉBOIST.

19.05 A la une

■ A la une demain, Joëlle MAZART. Reportage : Alain Herbeth.
■ A la une ce week-end. « Un fait d'hiver ». Reportage : Odile POUTGET.

19.20 Actualités régionales

19.45 Suspens

Émission proposée par Jacques ROULAND contée par Pierre BELLEMARE.
La Dame au téléphone. Le personnel du Casino.

19.53 Tirage de la Loterie nationale

Tranche Arlequin, en direct du Havre

20.00 TF 1 Actualités

20.35 Tirage du Loto

En direct du Havre

André DUSSOLLIER
joue actuellement
avec Caroline Cellier
et Sami Frey
TRAHISONS
d'Harold Pinter
au Théâtre Montparnasse

20.40 L'Epreuve

Pièce de MARIVAUX. Réalisation : Claude SANTELLI.
Lucidor, fils de riches marchands, vient d'acheter un château à la campagne. Malade, il est soigné par la gardienne, Madame Argante, dont la fille Angélique touche le cœur du jeune homme.
Malgré les attentions d'Angélique qui partage ses sentiments, Lucidor ne peut croire qu'elle l'aime. Il décide alors de l'éprouver en montant une machination.
Avec : André DUSSOLLIER (Lucidor), Magali RENOIR (Angélique), Jean-Luc MOREAU (Frontin), Jacques VILLERET (Blaise), Virginie PRADAL (Lisette), Tsilla CHELTON (Madame Argante).

Sunsitive les verres qui bronzent au soleil.

22.10 Les chercheurs du bout du monde

En Nouvelle-Calédonie, une centaine de chercheurs venus de monde entier, étudient, en coopération avec les Mélanésiens, premiers habitants de l'île, les plantes dont on peut extraire les médicaments. Un de ces médicaments qui s'est déjà révélé utile contre certains cancers du sein, sera bientôt commercialisé.

23.10 TF 1 Actualités

Demain sur TF 1
20.35 Veriétés :
« MUSIQUE, MÉLODIE »

---

a What sort of programme is on at 12.05 p.m.?
b At what time is the lunchtime news bulletin?
c Give **two** times at which you can see regional programmes?
d What type of programme is on at 4.30 p.m.?
e From which **two** programmes could you get information about holidays?
f At what time is the main evening news bulletin broadcast?
g For how long does this news bulletin last?
h From where is the draw for the National Lottery being transmitted?
i Is the draw being shown 'live' or recorded?
j At what time can you see a programme about research into the uses of plants?
k What type of programme is being shown at 8.40 p.m.?
l When can you see a magazine programme with items including cartoons and do-it-yourself tips?
m Give **one** other type of item in this magazine programme.

65

4

AVIS AUX JEUNES

Le Centre de Loisirs au 78, rue Nationale, Boulogne, vous rappelle que le centre fonctionne tous les mercredis de 14h. a 19h. Les activités suivantes y sont à votre disposition!

Cours de guitare (classique et moderne), débutants, et avancé.

Cours de danse moderne.
Cours de couture, broderie, photographie.
Atelier de peinture, dessin, poterie.
Sports: karaté, ping-pong, tennis (été seulement), football.

Le centre fonctionnera pendant toutes les vacances scolaires, les lundis, mardis, mercredis, jeudis, vendredis et samedis, de 14h. à 19h. Les activités seront les mêmes que pour les activités du mercredi.

Le Centre de Loisirs vous propose cette année un séjour en colonie de vacances pendant les vacances de Noël.
Ces vacances de neige auront lieu du 26 décembre (matin) au 3 janvier (soir).
Le prix extrêmement avantageux de 1260F permettra à tous de participer.
Sur simple appel téléphonique vous pouvez recevoir gratuitement notre brochure. Tel. 30.16.00.
Inscriptions au Centre tous les jours (sauf dimanche et lundi) de 10h. à 12h. et de 14h. à 18h.

a To whom is this announcement addressed?
b What lessons are available for music lovers?
c Name **two** other subjects in which lessons are available.
d Name **two** workshop activities available.
e What sports are offered?
f When is the Centre normally open?
g When is it open during school holidays?
h What type of holiday is the Centre offering during the Christmas period?
i How much will it cost? What is said about the price?
j What should you do if you want more information?
k When and where can you put your name down for this holiday?

5

DANS CE NUMERO POUR VOS T. SHIRTS
UN SUPER TRANSFERT

1. Choisissez un T-shirt de couleur claire.
Important : n'utilisez que du coton.
2. Posez le T-shirt à l'endroit sur une planche à repasser.
3. Réglez le fer sur coton et appliquez le transfert, côté imprimé, sur le T-shirt à l'endroit souhaité.
4. Posez votre fer, lorsqu'il a atteint la bonne température, sur le transfert et appuyez (20 secondes).
5. Otez le fer. Attendez 30 secondes. Vous n'avez plus qu'a soulever le papier.
6. Vous pouvez poser votre transfert au centre de votre T-shirt mais rien ne vous empêche d'innover en le mettant à un tout autre endroit.

Cet exemplaire de Salut ! n° 176 n'est complet qu'avec son transfert folioté p. 49. Si vous ne le trouviez pas à l'intérieur du journal, écrivez-nous: Salut ! « Réclamations », BP 87-08, 75360 Paris Cédex 08. N'omettez pas de joindre une enveloppe timbrée comportant votre adresse.

a What **two** things are you told about the type of T-shirt to choose?
b Where should you place the T-shirt?
c How long should you keep the iron on the transfer?
d What **two** things must you do when you have lifted off the iron?
e What exactly should you do if there is no transfer inside your copy of the magazine?

6

OFFRE SPECIALE

RESERVEE AUX LECTEURS DE SALUT!

Pour ceux qui désirent en savoir plus sur les vedettes qui ont fait le succès des années 60, recevez chez vous ce superbe livre cartonné de 140 pages illustrées de 100 photos couleurs et 35 noires.

60f. SEULEMENT

Réunies dans ce livre les plus belles photos des vedettes des annees 60, dont plusieurs sont encore au hit-parade de 82. Découvrez comment elles ont débuté dans la chanson grâce aux détails surprenants racontés par un journaliste de leurs amis qui vécut avec eux ces fabuleuses années 60. Un livre qui doit faire partie de la bibliothèque de ceux qui aiment la chanson.

BON DE COMMANDE

Je soussigné(e), désire recevoir le livre « Les idoles des années 60 » et je joins la somme de Frs : 60 F sous forme de :

☐ chèque bancaire ☐ chèque postal ☐ mandat-lettre à l'ordre de SONODIP
Nom : ....
Prénom : ....
Rue et N° : ....
Ville: .... Code postal : ....
Adressez le tout à SONODIP
BP 266 75264 PARIS CEDEX 06

a To whom is this special offer available?
b What is the book about?
c How many illustrations are there altogether?
d What information does the book give you?
e How was a journalist able to get this information?
f What is the exact title of the book?
g How much does it cost?

7

The following text is taken from the novel *Les Petits Enfants du Siècle* by Christiane Rochefort. The central character of the book is Josyane, the eldest child in a large working class family who live in the suburbs of Paris. She relates the story of her childhood and adolescence.
In this extract Josyane has just left school...

❮ Tout de suite, ce qui me manqua, c'était l'école. Pas tellement la classe elle-même, mais le chemin pour y aller, et, par-dessus tout, les devoirs. Peut-être qu'il existe au monde un métier où on fait ses devoirs toute sa vie. Je ne sais pas. Je me sentais inoccupée. Le soir, j'étais fatiguée, mes yeux se fermaient. Avant, le soir, je commençais à me réveiller, maintenant je tombais de sommeil.

L'hiver passa, le printemps revint. Maintenant, avec Liliane, Didier, Joël et les autres, on allait au cinéma. Du moment que la vaisselle était finie les parents me laissaient aller au cinéma, ils me donnaient même de l'argent, pour ça ils étaient gentils. Après tout je n'avais plus de devoirs, il fallait bien que je m'occupe, et le cinéma, je dois dire, remplaçait assez bien les devoirs. J'y serais allée tous les soirs, et tous les films sans exception me plaisaient. ❯

EITHER:
　Translate the passage into English.
OR:
　Answer in English the following questions:
a What did Josyane especially miss?
b How did she feel now in the evenings?
c How had she felt previously?
d In what way did her life change in the spring?
e When was she allowed to go out?
f In what way were her parents kind?
g Which type of films did Josyane like?

LISTENING COMPREHENSION

1

On a French radio programme, pupils of a CES (comprehensive school) were interviewed about their hobbies. Listen carefully to what they had to say before answering in English the following questions:

Thierry
a How old is he?
b Why does he say he is lucky?
c Why is it peaceful where he lives?
d How many hours a week does he devote to sport?

Chantal
a Where does she live?
b Name **two** activities she can pursue at the leisure centre.
c How many times a week does she go there?

Daniel
a How old is he?
b What is his unusual hobby?
c What does he say this hobby takes, as well as time?

Monique
a How old is she?
b When does she have piano lessons?
c What other instruments does she play?

Francine
a How often does she go to gymnastics class?
b When does she usually play volley-ball?
c What does she do at the weekend?

Luc
a Name **three** things he does after school.
b When does he go swimming?

2

Listen carefully to the passage before answering in English the following questions:
a On what date did the story take place?
b Where did Christophe and Armand live?
c At what time did they leave?
d What were they both carrying?
e What did Christophe have in his bag?
f Why did they decide to walk?
g Where did they sit down?
h Why did they choose that particular spot?
i What exactly did they catch during the morning?
j What did the boys do at 12.15 p.m.?
k What did Armand do afterwards?
l What did Christophe do at this time?
m Why did the two boys leave the river?
n How many fish had they caught?
o What were the people in the village doing?
p How did Christophe and Armand feel as they went through the village?
q What did the boys do before going to bed?

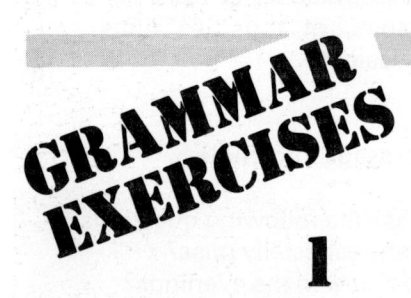

GRAMMAR EXERCISES

1

Translate into French the following sentences:
a She came to our house yesterday.
b I will do it myself.
c They (*m*) will go themselves.
d Chantal and Madeleine invited their friends to their house.
e She is younger than me.
f He is the one who broke the plate.
g You can do your homework yourself.

2

Copy the following passage putting each verb in brackets into the perfect tense:

Hier matin, Jean-Paul (téléphoner) à son amie Marianne, et il lui (demander) d'aller avec lui à une disco. Marianne (répondre): ‹Oui, d'accord.› Donc ils (se retrouver) à huit heures devant la mairie. Dans la discothèque, ils (voir) beaucoup d'amis. Ils (danser), ils (bavarder), et ils (boire) de la bière. Mais tout à coup le tourne-disques (s'arrêter). Quel dommage!
Deux garçons, Marc et Jean-Luc, (monter) dans leur vieille voiture et ils (aller) chercher leurs guitares.

‹Veux-tu chanter?› (dire) Marc à Jean-Paul, et Jean-Paul (chanter) avec eux. Tout le monde (s'amuser) bien. A onze heures et demie ils (partir). Jean-Paul et Marianne (courir), mais malheureusement ils (manquer) l'autobus, et ils (devoir) rentrer à pied. Ils (arriver) chez eux à minuit.

3

Rewrite the passage in exercise 2 as though it is being told by Jean-Paul. Make any other changes, as well as verbs, which are necessary. Begin it "Hier matin, j'ai téléphoné . . ."

TRAVAIL ORAL

EXAMPLE:
J'ai fait mes devoirs.

1 Look at the picture clues and say what you did yesterday evening.

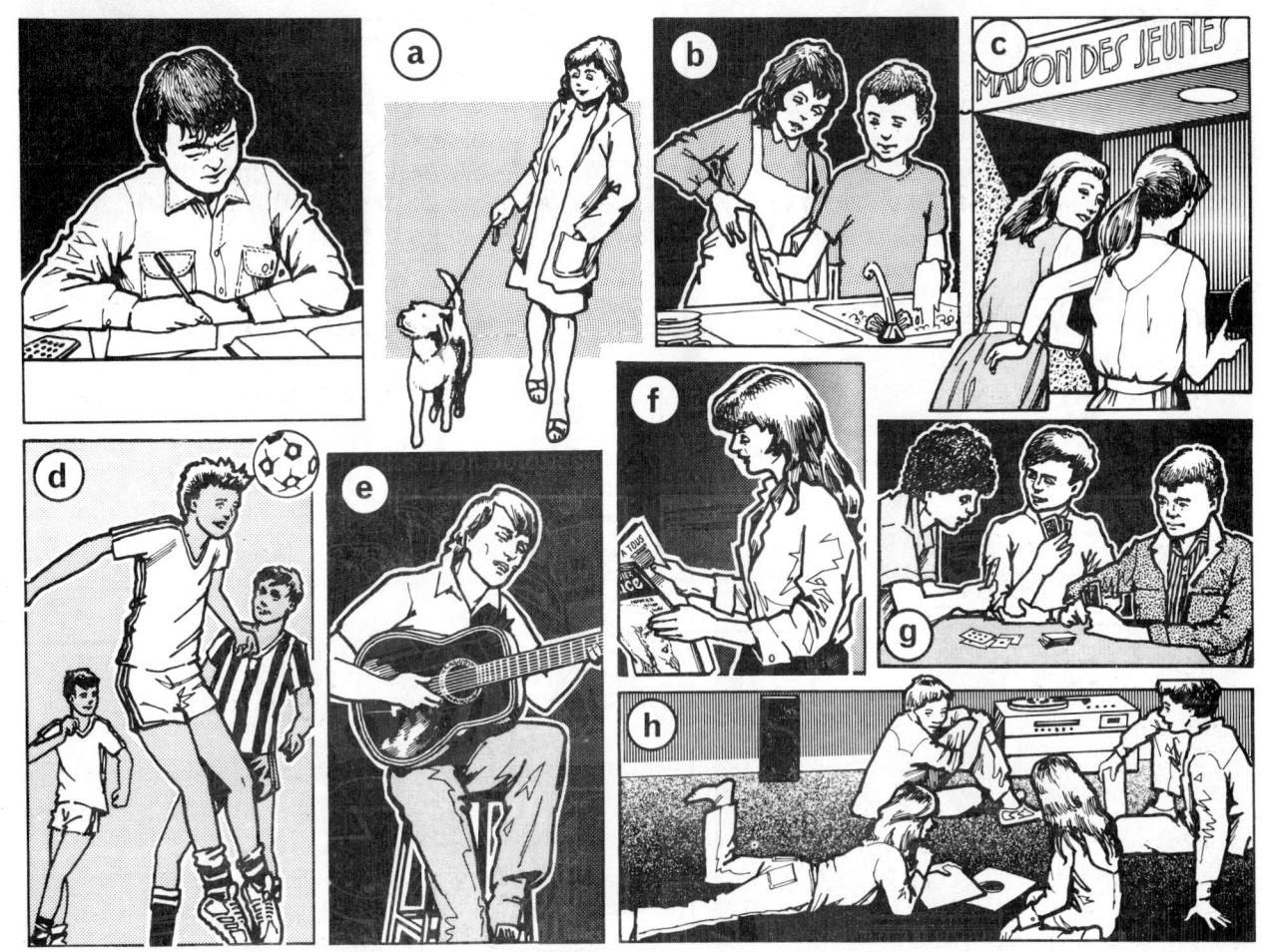

69

2

In the same way use the picture clues to say what you did last weekend, but this time say **two** sentences about each picture.

3

Imagine you are being interviewed in the same way as the French pupils in exercise 1 of the LISTENING COMPREHENSION. Say a few sentences about leisure facilities in your district, and what you do in your spare time.

TRAVAIL ECRIT

1

Write the answers to exercises 1 and 2 of the TRAVAIL ORAL section.

2

Using the present tense, write a letter to your French penfriend telling him/her how you usually spend your evenings and weekends. Ask your penfriend about his/her hobbies and leisure activities.

3

Choose one of the following titles and write a suitable essay, using past tenses:
a Une soirée à la Maison des Jeunes
b Une promenade à vélo
c Un après-midi à la piscine

4

Write a story which the following pictures suggest to you.
Remember to use past tenses.

VOCABULARY

Reading comprehension

1
devenir – to become
équipe (f) – team
instituteur (m) – primary school teacher
Manche (f) – English Channel
nageur (m) – swimmer
parmi – among
réussir – to succeed
tenter – to attempt
traversée (f) – crossing

2
chômage (m) – unemployment
chose (f) – thing
contre – against
état (m) – state
étranger – foreign
interdire – to forbid
mécanicien (m) – mechanic
pays (m) – country
podium (m) – platform
porter un coup – to strike a blow

3
actualités (f pl) – news
bricolage (m) – odd-jobbing, do-it-yourself
dessin (m) animé – cartoon
feuilleton (m) – serial
pièce (f) – play

4
avoir lieu – to take place
broderie (f) – embroidery
colonie (f) de vacances – holiday camp
couture (f) – needlework
dessin (m) – drawing
fonctionner – (here) to be open
peinture (f) – painting
suivant – following
vacances (f pl) scolaires – school holidays

5
appuyer – to press
clair – light
fer (m) – iron
ôter – to take off
planche (f) à repasser – ironing board

6
chanson (f) – song
débuter – to begin
lecteur (m)/lectrice (f) – reader
vedette (f) – star (of pop, cinema, etc.)

7
il fallait – it was necessary
laisser – to let, to allow
manquer – to miss
même – even
métier (m) – job
monde (m) – world
s'occuper – to occupy oneself, to keep busy
plaire – to please
remplacer – to replace
se sentir – to feel
sommeil (m) – sleep

Listening comprehension

1
activités (f pl) manuelles – handicrafts
argent (m) de poche – pocket money
centre (m) de loisirs – leisure centre
chance (f) – (good) luck
cimetière (m) – cemetery
être inscrit (à) – to be enrolled (at)
natation (f) – swimming
poissons (m pl) exotiques – tropical fish
plutôt – rather
situé – situated
spécial – unusual
tas (m) – (here) a lot

2
botte (f) – boot
canne (f) à pêche – fishing rod
content – pleased, happy
faire nuit – to get dark
ligne (f) – line
pêcher – to fish
rivière – river
ver (m) – worm

GRAMMAR

The perfect tense

The perfect tense is used for events which happened in the past. It is very important to learn this tense thoroughly, because it is the one you will need most often in your own writing. Remember that to form the perfect tense of any verb you need TWO WORDS. If you have written only one, it is WRONG!

Formation of the perfect tense using 'avoir'

The perfect tense is generally formed by using the present tense of the verb 'avoir' (to have) followed by the past participle of whatever verb you are using.
Here is the present tense of 'avoir':

j'ai	nous avons
tu as	vous avez
il a	ils ont
elle a	elles ont

Regular past participles are formed in the following way:

Infinitive	Past participle
donner – to give	donné
finir – to finish	fini
vendre – to sell	vendu

Here are some examples of verbs in the perfect tense:
j'ai donné — I gave, I have given
il a fini — he finished, he has finished
elle a parlé — she spoke, she has spoken
nous avons vendu — we sold, we have sold
ils ont choisi — they chose, they have chosen

Some verbs have past participles which are not formed according to the patterns above. They are **irregular**, and must be learnt by heart.

Here is a list of some of the commonest ones:

Infinitive	Past particple
avoir – to have	eu
boire – to drink	bu
courir – to run	couru
devoir – to have to, must	dû
dire – to say, to tell	dit
écrire – to write	écrit
être – to be	été
faire – to do, to make	fait
lire – to read	lu
mettre – to put, to put on	mis
ouvrir – to open	ouvert
pleuvoir – to rain	plu
prendre – to take	pris
pouvoir – to be able, can	pu
savoir – to know	su
suivre – to follow	suivi
tenir – to hold	tenu
voir – to see	vu
vouloir – to want	voulu

ALL THESE VERBS FORM THEIR PERFECT TENSE WITH AVOIR

Formation of the perfect tense using 'être'

There are thirteen verbs and their compounds which form their perfect tense by using the present tense of 'être' (to be) with the past participle.
These verbs are:

aller	venir (venu)
entrer	sortir
arriver	partir
monter	descendre
rester	retourner
naître (né)	mourir (mort)
tomber	

Here is the present tense of 'être':

je suis	nous sommes
tu es	vous êtes
il est	ils sont
elle est	elles sont

There is a most important difference about these thirteen verbs. The past participle must 'agree' (like an adjective) with its subject.
EXAMPLE:
il est allé   he went
BUT:
elle est allée   she went

ils sont allés   they went (*m*)
BUT:
elles sont allées   they went (*f*)

Look at these further examples:
il est parti
elle est partie
nous sommes sortis
Pierre et Alain sont restés
Marie et Marianne sont restées

Another group of verbs which take 'être' to form their perfect tense are all the **reflexive verbs**.

> Here is a list of common reflexive verbs:
> s'amuser – to enjoy oneself
> s'asseoir (assis) – to sit down
> se brosser les dents – to brush one's teeth
> se coucher – to go to bed
> se dépêcher – to hurry
> se fâcher – to get angry
> s'habiller – to get dressed
> se laver – to wash (oneself)
> se lever – to get up
> se peigner – to brush one's hair
> se promener – to go for a walk
> se réveiller – to wake up
> se sauver – to run away, to escape

Here is a reflexive verb in the perfect tense:
je me suis lavé   nous nous sommes lavés
tu t'es lavé   vous vous êtes lavé(s)
il s'est lavé   ils se sont lavés
elle s'est lavée   elles se sont lavées

● Notice that the past participle agrees, just as in other verbs which use 'être' in the perfect tense.

Negatives

You have already learned where to place the negative (ne . . . pas, ne . . . jamais, etc.) when using the perfect tense.

The following examples are a reminder of the rules:
Elle n'a pas entendu.
Nous ne sommes pas sortis.
Je ne l'ai jamais vu.
Il ne s'est pas levé.
Ils n'ont rien vu.
BUT:
Ils n'ont vu personne.

Some additional points about the perfect tense

1 The 'preceding direct object' (or PDO) rule
You have learned that with verbs which use 'avoir' in the perfect tense, the past participle does not agree, it remains unchanged. However, there is one type of sentence where this is not so.
EXAMPLE:
J'ai vu Pierre et Paul. (No agreement.)
BUT:
Je les ai vus. (Agreement with 'les', i.e. masculine plural, because it **precedes** the verb.)
Elle a acheté la robe blanche. (No agreement.)
Elle l'a achetée. (Agreement with l' which refers to 'la robe blanche' which is feminine singular.)
Nous avons acheté trois cartes postales. (No agreement.)
Nous les avons achetées. (Agreement with 'les' which refers to 'trois cartes postales', i.e. feminine plural.)

● Note that many of these changes are only apparent in written French. Remember to check your essays and letters for PDO agreements.
Sometimes, however, they show up in speaking – look at the following:
Tu as pris les assiettes? Oui, je les ai prises.
Où est ma montre? Je l'ai mise sur le buffet.

> **BUT REMEMBER THAT IN THE VAST MAJORITY OF CASES THERE IS NO AGREEMENT OF THE PAST PARTICIPLE IN VERBS WHICH TAKE AVOIR – ONLY WHEN THERE IS A PRECEDING DIRECT OBJECT.**

2 Reflexive verbs

You have learnt that reflexive verbs take 'être' in the perfect tense, and that the past participle must 'agree'. This is because the reflexive pronoun is, in fact, a preceding direct object.
EXAMPLE:
Elle s'est lavée   She washed herself.
'lavée' agrees with 's' – herself

Occasionally, however, the reflexive pronoun is not the direct object.
EXAMPLE:
Elle s'est lavé les mains.   She washed her hands.
Here, the direct object is 'les mains', therefore, since the reflexive pronoun 's'' is not a direct object, there is no agreement.

● Note that although the verbs 'monter', 'descendre', 'sortir', 'rentrer', usually take 'être' in the perfect tense, they take 'avoir' if they have a direct object.
EXAMPLE:
Elle a monté l'escalier sur la pointe des pieds.
She went upstairs on tiptoe.

J'ai descendu les valises de la chambre.
I brought the suitcases down from the bedroom.

Tout à coup, le cambrioleur a sorti un revolver.
Suddenly the burglar took out a revolver.

Nous avons rentré les chaises du jardin, car il va pleuvoir.
We've brought in the chairs from the garden because it's going to rain.

Pluperfect tense

This tense is used where, in English, we use 'had' with a past participle.
EXAMPLE:
I had done, he had seen, they had arrived

If you have thoroughly understood the rules about the perfect tense, you will have no difficulty in forming the pluperfect tense. It is exactly the same as the perfect tense, except that you use the **imperfect tense** of 'avoir' or 'être' with a past participle.
EXAMPLE:
j'avais donné   I had given
il avait fini   he had finished
nous avions vendu   we had sold
ils avaient pris   they had taken
elle était allée   she had gone
ils s'étaient levés   they had got up

Emphatic pronouns

The following are known as 'emphatic' or 'disjunctive' pronouns.
They are used as follows:

1 **Alone, in answer to a question**
EXAMPLE:
Qui est là? Moi.   Who is there?. I.
2 **As the second term of a comparison**
EXAMPLE:
Elle est plus jeune que toi.   She is younger than you.

3 **After prepositions**
EXAMPLE:
avec moi   with me
sans eux   without them
4 **After 'chez'**
EXAMPLE:
chez elle   at her house
chez nous   at our house
5 **After the verb 'être'**
EXAMPLE:
C'est vous qui avez mangé le denier gâteau.
You are the one who ate the last cake.
6 **With 'même' – meaning myself, yourself, etc.**
EXAMPLE:
Tu peux le faire toi-même.   You can do it yourself.
Ils font la cuisine eux-mêmes.   They do the cooking themselves.

REVISION TEST ONE

Grammar

1 The pictures on the left show what Alain used to do. Those on the right show what he does now. Write a sentence for each picture. Look carefully at the examples first.

EXAMPLE:
Il allait à l'école primaire

EXAMPLE:
Il va au collège

2

Rewrite these sentences, replacing the word (or words) in capital letters with the correct pronoun:

a Je connais bien PAUL.
b Il a deux CRAYONS.
c Le professeur parle AUX ELEVES.
d J'ai téléphoné A SYLVIE hier soir.
e Tu as vu Pierre? Oui, J'ai vu PIERRE samedi dernier.
f J'aime bien la campagne, donc je vais A LA CAMPAGNE tous les weekends.
g Tu as apporté des disques? Oui, j'ai apporté DES DISQUES.
h Ne mettez pas LES CAHIERS sur la table, mettez LES CAHIERS dans le placard.
i Donnez-moi LA VALISE et je mettrai LA VALISE dans la voiture.

3

Rewrite these sentences putting the infinitive in brackets into the perfect tense:

a Je (recevoir) une belle montre pour mon anniversaire.
b Nous (partir) de bonne heure.
c Il (dire) 'Au revoir' à sa mère.
d Josyane (boire) un verre de limonade.
e Je (mettre) les oeufs dans le frigo.
f Quand nous (voir) ce grand chien nous (avoir) peur.
g Ma grand-mère (naître) en 1920.
h Nous (écrire) des cartes postales.
i Jean et Philippe (faire) la vaisselle.
j Papa (vendre) notre vieille voiture.
k Ma tante (venir) nous voir dimanche passé.
l Ma petite soeur (tomber) dans le jardin.
m Marie et Françoise (se coucher) assez tard.
n Nous (s'amuser) bien à la Maison des Jeunes.
o Il (devoir) courir pour prendre l'autobus.
p La vieille Madame Durand (mourir) il y a deux ans.

4

Write in French:

a We are not listening to the radio.
b I didn't understand.
c It was not very cold.
d I didn't see him yesterday.
e I'm sorry, there are no more apples.
f She has only one brother.
g I met nobody.
h They heard nothing.
i He never goes out without his dog.
j Don't get up ('tu' form) too late.

5

Write in French:

a Where are you going?
b How many brothers have you got?
c When are you coming to see us?
d Why have you put on that old shirt?
e Have you seen Paul?
f Is your mother in the garden?
g At what time do you get up?
h When did he leave?
i Will you be at home this evening?
j How are you?

Vocabulary

In the following groups you must match each word with its correct meaning:

1

le fauteuil	to break down
le canapé	the corner
l'armoire	to move house
l'immeuble	the stairs
tomber en panne	the suburbs
l'escalier	the armchair
déménager	the wardrobe
l'échelle	the block of flats
le coin	the ladder
la banlieue	the settee

2

mélanger	the glasses
le copain	the recipe
prendre un verre	to mix
le maquillage	the plate
les lunettes	the bowl
la recette	the friend
l'assiette	to add
le bol	the dust
ajouter	to have a drink
la poussière	the make-up

77

3

la note	the season ticket
aîné	the timetable
le cours	the subject
se moquer de	the mark
l'emploi du temps	the nursery school
la cloche	to hurry
la carte d'abonnement	elder
la matière	the lesson
la maternelle	to make fun of
se dépêcher	the bell

4

le porte-monnaie	to save
le prix	the bookshop
le sparadrap	a public holiday
la fermeture	the beef
économiser	the vegetable
la librairie	roast
la quincaillerie	the veal
un jour férié	the purse
le boeuf	the trout
le veau	the elastoplast
le légume	the hardware shop
rôti	the closure
la truite	the price

5

l'équitation	the team
le poisson	the cartoon
fatigué	the news
la canne à pêche	horse riding
l'équipe	the serial
le dessin animé	the bicycle
le feuilleton	the fish
les actualités	tired
la piscine	the fishing rod
le vélo	the swimming pool

DOSSIER 6
EN VACANCES

READING COMPREHENSION

1

Sac à nouvelles

Cinémas : au Stella, ce soir à 21 h 15, "Les uns et les autres". Demain, même heure, "Le cadeau".
Au Lido : ce soir, à 21 h 30 "L'homme de Prague". Demain, même heure, "Un justicier dans la ville".
En balade : demain, l'agence Viarama vous propose une excursion à Carcassonne (départ 8 h 30), et l'après-midi, une visite de Saint-Martin du Canigou (départ 13 h 40).
Antic-Auto-club catalan : aujourd'hui à 17 h, les vieux tacots de nos grands-pères (et grands-mères) défileront dans les rues de la station. A partir de 18 h, place de la Méditerranée, concours d'élégance.

Piscine : elle est à votre disposition à côté de la capitainerie du port. Ouverte tous les jours de 9 h à 19 h.
Pour se déplacer : vous pouvez louer à la capitainerie des voitures electriques. Pour les conduire, le permis B est nécessaire. Tarif horaire : 60 F. Pour la journée, il vous en coûtera 220 F.
Location de vélos au syndicat d'initiative, à la capitainerie du port, au marché du centre, à la mairie et dans les campings. Tarif journalier : 15 F.
Deux roues : l'Amicale cyclotouriste organise tous les jours des randonnées à bicyclette. Départ tous les matins à 7 h 30 et 8 h, devant le marchand de cycles Zublena.
Sorties en mer : le club de pêche organise tous les jours des sorties en mer pour tous. Inscriptions à la capitainerie du port.
Tennis : il existe quatre courts découverts sur la station situés à côté de la poste. Ils sont ouverts de 7 h à minuit. Réservations sur place, 24 heures à l'avance. Tarif horaire 35 F. D'autre part, vous pouvez prendre des leçons ou suivre des stages. Renseignements sur place.
Syndicat d'initiative : pour des renseignements complémentaires, s'adresser au syndicat d'initiative, place de la Méditerranée, tél. 80.20.65.

a What is the title of the film showing tomorrow at the Stella cinema?
b At what time does the film begin?
c When exactly is there an excursion to Saint-Martin du Canigou?
d When is the swimming pool open?
e To hire an electric car, what is:
  i the hourly rate?
  ii the rate per day?
f Name **two** places where you can hire bicycles.
g Where must you meet if you want to go on the cycling excursion?
h Which club organises sea trips?
i Where are the tennis courts?
j How do you make reservations?
k What is the cost of hiring a court?

2

OÙ AIMERAIS-TU ALLER EN VACANCES, CETTE ANNÉE : MER OU MONTAGNE?

TU SAIS, JE CROIS QUE TOI ET MOI N'AURONS PAS LE CHOIX...

MAMAN A ACHETÉ HIER SIX MAILLOTS DE BAINS!

a What choice of holiday places is the father suggesting to his son?
b What is the son's reply?
c What reason does he give for his answer?
d Write down from the captions examples of:
  i the present tense;
  ii the future tense;
  iii the conditional tense;
  v the perfect tense.

3

Profitez de vos vacances à Annecy!
Faites des excursions!

LES AUTOCARS DE SAVOIE vous propose :

TOUR DU LAC D'ANNECY – t.l.j. sauf lundi.
Départ 14 h 00 Retour 16 h 30
Prix 20 F. Enf. 12F.

JOURNEE DANS LES ALPES – mardi, vendredi, (sauf jours fériés)
Chamonix, Mégève. Prix 50F. Enf. 30F.
Ascension du Mont Blanc en téléférique 15F supp.
Départ 10 h 00 Retour 18 h 00.

JOURNEE EN SUISSE – jeudi (sauf 15 août)
Evian (arrêt 30 minutes), Montreux (arrêt 1 heure), Genève (arrêt 2 heures). Passeport nécessaire.
Prix 80F. Enf. 50F.
Visite de Genève avec guide (durée 1 heure) 15F supp.
Excursion en bateau sur le Lac Léman (durée 45 minutes) 18F supp.
Depart 9 h 30. Retour 19 h 30.

Locations au bureau des Autocars de Savoie, 10, Av. Rousseau Annecy

ouvert t.l.j. (sauf dimanche) 9 h 00 à 19 h 30.

a From which French town does this firm operate?
b Where exactly can you book tickets and at what times?
c On which of the following days can you **not** take the tour round Lake Annecy: Thursday; Sunday; Monday?
d On which days can you take the excursion to the Alps? What are the exceptions?
e How long does the Alps excursion last?
f How much will it cost two adults, if they want to go up Mont Blanc as well?
g What do you need for the Swiss excursion?
h How long is the stop in Evian?
i How much will the trip cost a family consisting of a mother, father and two children, without any extras?
j Give **two** details about the visit to Geneva.
k How much does the boat trip cost and how long does it last?

4

GUIDE TOURISTIQUE

CANET – Son petit port de pêche, ses plages magnifiques, ses forêts de pin, sa vieille place, ses vieilles maisons, son passé historique, ses distractions – font de Canet la ville idéale pour vos vacances.

Le PORT DE PECHE: Le coeur de notre petite ville. Vous y trouverez nos sympathiques cafés où vous pourrez déguster nos excellentes crêpes.

Les PLAGES: Des kilomètres de sable fin, des plages propres. Baignade surveillée par maîtres-nageurs avec poste de secours à proximité.

La VILLE les MAGASINS: Si vous aimez le shopping, visitez la vieille ville et ses rues piétonnes. Vous y trouverez des spécialités régionales, ses tissages à l'ancienne et aussi ses boutiques à la mode.

LES DISTRACTIONS: Nombreuses et variées!
Pour les jeunes et les moins jeunes!
Jeux de plage organisés, club de gymnastique pour enfants et adultes sur la plage, pédalos, tennis, golf, ping-pong, volley-ball etc. au Centre aéré de Loisirs près de la plage dans la forêt du Guitou. Promenades à cheval dans la forêt de pin.

Le SOIR: Nombreux divertissements et spectacles au Casino. Cabaret, chanteurs, grands spectacles de prestidigitation. Consulter la presse locale.

Renseignements Utiles:

Syndicat d'Initiative: Maison de la vieille lanterne. Place du grand Marché. Permanence de 8 h à 20 h. Ouv. le dimanche matin de 9 h à midi.

Banques: Ouvertes de 9 h à 17 h sans interruption, ts les jours sauf Samedi, Dimanche. – En août permanence le samedi matin de 10 h à midi.

Campings Municipaux: Camping du Phare – 3 étoiles, sur la falaise, vue étonnante sur la baie du port. Tout confort. Camping de la Rade – 2 étoiles, très confortable, jeux organisés pour les enfants.

---

a Name **three** attractions of Canet.
b What could you eat at cafés near the harbour?
c State **one** advantage of the beaches.
d Where would you find pedestrian only streets?
e Name **four** possible daytime activities.
f What are you advised to do to find out what is on during the evenings?
g During which months are the banks open on Saturday mornings?
h Which camp site would be more suitable for children?

5

Bordeaux, le 15 avril

Cher Ian,

J'ai bien reçu ta dernière lettre que tu as postée à Norwich mardi dernier, et je suis très heureux de savoir que tu veux bien faire un échange avec moi cet été.

J'ai une bonne nouvelle pour toi. Cet été mes parents prennent leurs vacances au mois d'août, et si ta famille est d'accord, nous t'invitons à nous accompagner à Biarritz. Tu verras que c'est vraiment formidable! Mes parents ont une caravane, mais nous deux, nous pourrons dormir sous la tente. Est-ce que tu as déjà fait du camping? Il faudra bien faire la vaisselle de temps en temps, et préparer les légumes! J'espère que cela ne t'ennuiera pas.

Heureusement nous aurons beaucoup d'autres occupations bien plus agréables. Si tu aimes pêcher, mon père nous emmènera en bateau et mon frère Jacques te prêtera une de ses cannes à pêche - il en a trois.

La plage est à deux kilomètres du camping et nous avons l'habitude d'y faire des parties de volley avec toute une bande de camarades que nous retrouvons au même camping chaque année.

J'espère que tu sais bien nager parce que c'est l'un des sports que nous pratiquons le plus en été. Nous organisons de temps en temps des compétitions entre nous. C'est toujours Jacques qui gagne, parce qu'il est très fort et s'entraîne régulièrement en piscine. Mais cette année je compte bien le battre et j'espère que tu seras là pour assister à ma victoire.

Le moment que je préfère c'est celui du feu de camp. Tu peux imaginer la scène...lorsque la nuit tombe, nous nous réunissons autour d'un feu de bois, et tandis que les uns s'occupent d'y faire griller des saucisses, les autres discutent, bavardent et chantent en s'accompagnant d'une guitare. Sais-tu jouer de la guitare? Moi, j'ai pris deux leçons de guitare, mais j'ai arrêté, parce que j'ai trouvé ça trop difficile.

Dépêche-toi de me répondre et de me dire si tes parents sont d'accord avec ce projet. Tu pourras venir le 3 août et rester jusqu'à la fin du mois.

Amitiés,

Jean-Marc

a When did Ian post his last letter to Jean-Marc?
b What invitation did Jean-Marc make to Ian in the second paragraph? (Give all relevant details.)
c What **two** household chores will Ian have to do from time to time?
d In what way would Jean-Marc's father and brother each help the boys with their fishing trip?
e What is said about the friends who play volley-ball with Jacques and Jean-Marc on the beach?
f State **two** of the reasons why Jacques is a good swimmer.
g What does Jean-Marc hope that he will be able to do while Ian is there this summer?
h How do the boys or their friends grill sausages?
i What does Jean-Marc say about his guitar lessons? (Give **two** details.)
j When does Jean-Marc suggest that Ian returns home after his visit to France?

LA METEO ASSEZ BIEN ENSOLEILLE

REGION PARISIENNE
Des nuages et des éclaicies le matin avec risque de quelques petites pluies orageuses locales. L'après-midi, il fera assez beau, avec de belles périodes ensoleillées. Température maximale de l'ordre de 20° à 22°.

AILLEURS
De la Bretagne au Nord, nuages et éclaircies alterneront, et quelques averses sont possibles près de la Manche. Encore des orages isolés de l'Alsace à la Provence.
Sur les autres régions, temps brumeux en matinée, avec des brouillards dans l'Ouest, puis généralement ensoleillé l'après-midi. Vents faibles. Températures de 19° dans le Nord du pays, à 25° dans le Midi.

DEMAIN
De la Bretagne à la frontière belge, temps souvent très nuageux avec des pluies intermittentes.
Sur les autres régions, temps brumeux le matin dans l'intérieur, puis assez ensoleillé dans la journée mais quelques nuages sur le sud-ouest et près de l'Atlantique. Températures stationnaires.

6

a What will the weather be like in the Paris area during
  i the morning?
  ii the afternoon?
b What type of weather is forecast for the north?
c Where are showers likely to occur?
d What type of weather is likely in other regions during the morning?
e Where is fog likely to occur?
f What will the highest temperature be, and in what part of the country?
g State **two** things you are told about the weather tomorrow from Brittany northwards.
h Where will there be a few clouds?
i What are you told about tomorrow's temperatures?

LISTENING COMPREHENSION

1

Listen carefully to the article before answering in English the following questions:
a How many workers are involved?
b When will their strike begin?
c What will be the result for travellers?
d At what season of the year is this taking place?
e For how long have these workers been protesting?
f What **two** things are they protesting about?

2

Listen carefully to the announcement before answering in English the following questions:
a To whom exactly is this announcement addressed?
b On which days is it preferable to leave?
c Between which times should you not travel on Saturday?
d Which people are advised to avoid the centre of Toulouse, and why?

3

Listen carefully to the passage before answering in English the following questions:
a For how long had the Duponts been looking for a country house?
b What did they call their cottage?
c Why had it taken them such a long time to save enough money?
d How many married children did they have?
e Why did the size of the house seem ideal?
f How far was the cottage from their town house?
g When would they leave for their cottage?
h How long did it take them to reach the cottage?
i Why didn't they go faster on Sunday evenings?
j What does Monsieur Dupont suggest they should do?

84

GRAMMAR

1 Write sentences to say how these people intend to go on holiday. Use the future tense of the verb 'aller' for a – g.

a Monsieur Durand

b Mademoiselle Favert

c Monsieur et Madame Laporte

d Jacques et Paul

e Francine et Sylvie

f Madame Leroy

g Christine et Chantal

h Mais nous ferons

85

2 Copy the letter below, putting each verb in brackets into the **future** tense.

Chère Suzanne,
    Merci pour ta gentille lettre. Tu me demandes mes projets de vacances, et quand je (pouvoir) venir te voir. Eh bien, je vais te (dire).

D'abord, j'(aller) chez ma tante, qui a été très malade. Je (faire) le ménage et je (préparer) les repas. L'après-midi, on (faire) les courses ensemble, et on (prendre) le thé dans un café. Le soir, après le souper, on (regarder) la télévision, et on (se coucher) de bonne heure. Après huit jours, mon père (venir) me chercher en voiture, et nous (rentrer) ensemble.

Ensuite, j'(aller) faire du camping en Écosse avec mes amis. J'espère que nous (avoir) beau temps. Nous (être) un groupe de six, trois garçons et trois filles. Les garçons (dresser) les tentes et (chercher) du bois pour le feu. Nous, les filles, nous (faire) les repas. Pour faire la vaisselle, je ne sais pas, on (voir) ! On (revenir/rentrer) d'Écosse vers le vingt août.

Après, je (pouvoir) venir passer quelques jours chez toi, comme tu m'as demandé. Si tu es d'accord, j'(arriver) le vingt-deux, et je (être) obligée de repartir le vingt-neuf, car mes cours (recommencer) le premier septembre. Est-ce que tes parents te (permettre) de venir en Angleterre avec moi ?

Écris-moi bientôt,
                    Sandra.

TRAVAIL ORAL

1

Look at the picture and answer the questions which follow.

a Est-ce que la dame rentre de vacances?
b Qu'est-ce qu'elle porte comme vêtements?
c Combien de valises voyez-vous?
d Combien de boîtes voyez-vous?
e Qu'est-ce qu'elle va apprendre à son chien?
f Donnez un conseil à cette dame.

Regarde bien, je vais te montrer comment ouvrir les boîtes pendant que je serai en vacances.

2

Answer according to the instructions given in each of the following interviews.

INTERVIEW 1

a Qu'est-ce que tu vas faire pendant les grandes vacances?
(*Say you are going camping with some friends.*)
b Où allez-vous?
(*Say you are going to the Bellevue campsite near La Baule.*)
c C'est près de la plage?
(*Say yes, it's near the beach, and also there is a swimming pool at the camp site.*)
d Qu'est-ce qu'il y a d'autre à ce camping?
(*Say there is a shop, a restaurant and tennis courts.*)
e Et s'il pleut?
(*Say there is a games room and a television room.*)
f Alors, bonnes vacances!
(*Say thank you.*)

INTERVIEW 2

a Qu'est-ce que tu vas faire pendant les vacances de Pâques?
(*Say you are going to spend a week with your French penfriend.*)
b Où est-ce qu'il/elle habite, ton/ta correspondant(e)?
(*Say he/she lives at Menton, near the Italian frontier.*)
c Et qu'est-ce que tu vas faire pendant ton séjour?
(*Say you are going on an excursion to Monte Carlo.*)
d Et autre chose?
(*Say you are going to spend a day in Italy.*)
e Tu as de la chance! Bonnes vacances!
(*Say thank you.*)

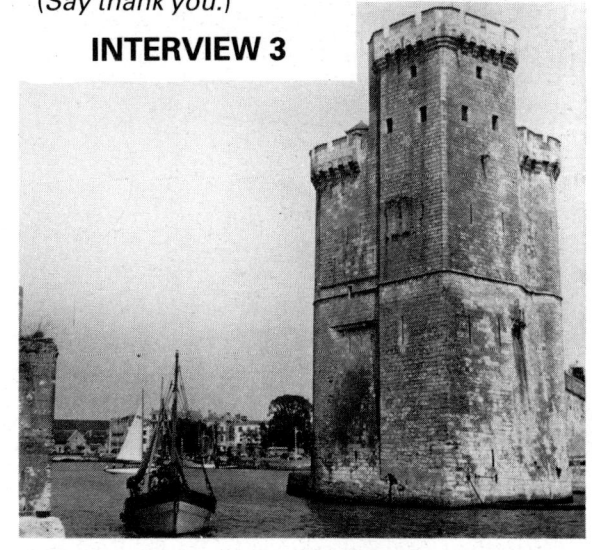

INTERVIEW 3

a Qu'est-ce que tu as fait pendant les grandes vacances?
(*Say you spent a fortnight with your parents near La Rochelle.*)
b Vous avez loué une villa?
(*Say no, you stayed at a hotel.*)
c Tu as aimé La Rochelle?
(*Say yes, it' a beautiful town. You liked the old port very much.*)
d Vous avez fait des excursions?
(*Say yes, you went on a trip to the Ile de Ré.*)
e Est-ce qu'il a fait beau temps?
(*Say no, it rained every day.*)
f Qu'est-ce que tu vas faire l'année prochaine pendant les grandes vacances?
(*Say you are going to Spain – it's hot there!*)

TRAVAIL ECRIT

Study carefully the following two letters before doing the exercises.

---

79 Hillview House
Castle Estate
ALLBOROUGH

le 14 avril

Monsieur G Favart
Directeur
Camping Les Pins
Belleville-sur-mer

Monsieur

Je voudrais retenir un emplacement pour une caravane et une voiture pour quinze jours à partir du premier juillet. J'aimerais savoir vos tarifs.

J'attends confirmation de votre part.

Veuillez agréer, Monsieur, l'expression de mes sentiments distingués.

M Fortune

---

17 Lockwood Road
NEWTOWN

le 3 mai

Monsieur G Belfort
Directeur
Hotel Beauséjour
Concarneau

Monsieur

Je voudrais retenir une chambre à deux lits avec salle de bains, et une chambre à un lit avec douche, à partir du 16 juillet jusqu'au 2 août. J'aimerais savoir vos tarifs pour les chambres avec demi-pension.

J'attends confirmation de votre part.

Veuillez agréer, Monsieur, l'expression de mes sentiments distingués.

P Finch

1
Write to the Hôtel Bellevue at La Baule. Reserve a double room with shower from 9th to 16th August. Ask the price of the room with full board (la pension complète).

2
Write to the camp site Sable d'Or at Leucate. Book a site for two tents and a car for three weeks from 28th July.

3
Write to the Hôtel du Commerce at Dieppe. Book two double rooms with bathrooms for the night of 17th August. Say you will arrive about 6.30 in the evening and will want dinner at the hotel.

4
Write a letter to your French penfriend, telling him/her what you did during the summer holidays

5
Write a letter to your French penfriend, inviting him/her to stay with you during the Easter holidays. Suggest some things you could do during the visit.

6
Write a reply to the letter in exercise 5. Accept the invitation, say when and where you will arrive. Ask if you need to bring warm clothes. Mention some of the things you would like to see and do during your visit.

7 Write a story which the pictures suggest to you.

1. GATWICK
2.
3. PARIS ORLY
4. DOUANE — Contrôle de Passports
5. HOTEL BEAUPRE — TAXI
6. ACCUEIL — ASCENSEUR

VOCABULARY

Reading comprehension

1
à côté de – beside, next to
demain – tomorrow
horaire – (here) hourly
location (f) – hiring
louer – to hire, rent
mairie (f) – townhall
même – same
randonnée (f) – outing, trip
sur place – on the spot
syndicate (m) d'initiative – tourist information office
tarif (m) – rate

2
choix (m) – choice
maillot (m) de bain – swimming costume
mer (f) – sea
montagne (f) – mountain

3
durée (f) – duration
jour (m) férié – public holiday

89

location *(f)* – hire, rent
sauf – except

4

baignade *(f)* – bathing
chanteur *(m)* – singer
crêpe *(f)* – pancake
déguster – to taste
distraction *(f)* – amusement
divertissement *(m)* – amusement
étoile *(f)* – star
falaise *(f)* – cliff
gratuit – free of charge
jeu *(m)* – game
maître-nageur *(m)* – lifeguard
piscine *(f)* – swimming pool
piéton – pedestrian (noun *(m)* & adj)
pin *(m)* – pine tree
plage *(f)* – beach
poste *(m)* de secours – first aid post
propre – clean
à proximité – nearby
sable *(m)* – sand
spectacle *(m)* – show
surveillé – supervised

5

assister à – to be present at
bande *(f)* – group, gang
bateau *(m)* – boat
battre – to beat
camarade *(m)* – friend
canne *(f)* à pêche – fishing rod
compter – to count (on)
de temps en temps – from time to time
emmener – to take out, to take away, (people)
échange *(m)* – exchange
espérer – to hope
être d'accord – to agree
(il) faudra – (it) will be necessary
fort – strong
gagner – to win
habitude *(f)* – habit
heureusement – fortunately
lorsque – when
mois *(m)* – month
nager – to swim
nouvelle *(f)* – (piece of) news
prêter – to lend
projet *(m)* – plan
se réunir – to meet
tandis que – while
tomber – to fall

6

ailleurs – elsewhere
averse *(f)* – shower
brouillard *(m)* – fog
brume *(f)* – mist
brumeux – misty
couvert – overcast
éclaircie *(f)* – clear period
faible – light (of winds)
fort – strong (of winds)
frais – fresh
matinal – in the morning
nuage *(m)* – cloud
nuageux – cloudy
pluie *(f)* – rain

Listening comprehension

1

entraîner – to produce, to cause
estival – summer (adj)
grève *(f)* – strike
marin *(m)* – sailor
personnel *(m)* – staff
réduire – to reduce
retard *(m)* – delay
salaire *(m)* – wages
traverser – to cross

2

conseil *(m)* – advice
embouteillage *(m)* – traffic jam
éviter – to avoid
obligé – obliged, forced to
sud *(m)* – south
suivant – following

3

assez – enough
attendre – to wait
circulation *(f)* – traffic
se demander – to wonder
économiser – to save
élever – to bring up
gagner – to earn
loin – far
mériter – to deserve
quarantaine *(f)* – about forty
repos *(m)* – rest
résidence *(f)* – second secondaire (holiday) home
rêver – to dream
sembler – to seem
ville *(f)* – town

GRAMMAR

The future tense

The future tense in French translates the English I will . . . or, I shall . . .

To form the future tense of regular verbs, take the infinitive (with —re verbs drop the final 'e'), then add the following endings:

—ai   —ons
—as   —ez
—a   —ont

Here is an example of each type of verb in the future tense.

```
                donner – to give
    je donnerai    I will give, I shall give
    tu donneras
    il donnera
    nous donnerons
    vous donnerez
    ils donneront
```

```
                finir – to finish
    je finirai    I will finish, I shall finish
    tu finiras
    il finira
    nous finirons
    vous finirez
    ils finiront
```

```
                vendre – to sell
    je vendrai    I will sell, I shall sell
    tu vendras
    il vendra
    nous vendrons
    vous vendrez
    ils vendront
```

Irregular verbs

These have the same future endings, but the stem to which they are added is irregular, i.e. it is not the infinitive.

The following common irregular verbs in the future tense should be learned by heart:

aller	j'irai	I shall go
avoir	j'aurai	I shall have
devoir	je devrai	I shall have to
envoyer	j'enverrai	I shall send
être	je serai	I shall be
faire	je ferai	I shall do/make
mourir	je mourrai	I shall die
pouvoir	je pourrai	I shall be able
savoir	je saurai	I shall know
tenir	je tiendrai	I shall hold
venir	je viendrai	I shall come
voir	je verrai	I shall see
vouloir	je voudrai	I shall want

The conditional tense

The conditional tense is formed by adding the imperfect endings (—ais, etc.) to the future stem of the verb.
EXAMPLE:

Future	**Conditional**
je donnerai	je donnerais
je finirai	je finirais
je vendrai	je vendrais

Verbs which have an irregular stem in the future tense have the same stem in the conditional tense.
EXAMPLE:

Future	**Conditional**
j'irai	j'irais
je ferai	je ferais

The conditional tense **is** used:

1 To translate English 'would' or 'should'.
EXAMPLE:
Il serait content de vous voir.
He would be pleased to see you.

Je voudrais une livre de pêches, s'il vous plaît.
I would like a pound of peaches, please.

Tu devrais aller voir ta tante.
You should (ought to) go and see your aunt.

2 To replace the future in indirect (reported) speech.
EXAMPLE:
Il a dit: 'J'arriverai (future) à six heures.'
Il a dit qu'il arriverait (conditional) à six heures.

3 In sentences with 'si' (if).
EXAMPLE:
Si tu étais gentil tu aiderais ta mère.
If you were kind, you would help your mother.
(Note: Si + imperfect + conditional.)

● NOTE
The conditional tense **is not** used:
When 'would' = 'wanted to'.
EXAMPLE:
The boy wouldn't answer
Le garçon ne voulait pas répondre.

When 'would' = 'used to'.
EXAMPLE:
He would leave the house at seven o'clock every day.
Il quittait la maison à sept heures tous les jours.

Après avoir + past participle

This is a simple and very useful construction. You should learn it thoroughly and try to use it in your essays.
EXAMPLE:
Après avoir fini son café, il est sorti.
Having finished (after finishing) his coffee he went out.

Après avoir lu le journal j'ai écouté des disques.
After reading the newspaper I listened to some records.

Après avoir joué au football ils ont pris une douche.
After playing football they had a shower.

This same construction can also be used with verbs which take 'être' in the perfect tense.
EXAMPLE:
Après être restée trois jours au lit elle se sentait mieux.
After staying in bed for three days she felt better.

Après s'être levés ils ont allumé un feu.
After getting up they lit a fire.

- You can see from the above examples that the same rules of agreement apply as for the perfect tense with 'être'.

Prepositions

Using prepositions correctly is one of the most difficult tasks in learning a foreign language. In this, and the dossiers which follow, you will find lists of common phrases and expressions with prepositions. These must be learnt thoroughly. Then try to use them as much as possible in your oral and written work.

Countries

'In' or 'to' a country in French is usually 'en'. This applies to all countries which are feminine (the majority).
en France   in France
en Angleterre   in England
en Espagne   in Spain
en Allemagne   in Germany

- We also use 'en' for provinces of France.
  en Bretagne   in Brittany
  en Provence   in Provence

The commonest exceptions to the countries rule are:
au Canada   in Canada
au Maroc   in Morocco
au Portugal   in Portugal
au Danemark   in Denmark
aux Etats-Unis   in the United States

Towns

There is no problem here. 'In' or 'to' a town is almost always 'à'.
à Paris   in Paris
à Londres   in London
à Moscou   in Moscow

- NOTE
  au Havre   to or in Le Havre
  au Mans   to or in Le Mans

Transport

à pied   on foot
à vélo/bicyclette   by bicycle
à cheval   on horseback, or astride
en voiture/auto   by car
en taxi   by taxi
en autocar   by coach
en avion   by plane
par le bateau   by boat
par le train   by train

Holiday and travel expressions

en ville   in (the) town
à la campagne   in the country
au bord de la mer   at the seaside
à la montagne   in the mountains
à la plage   on the beach
au soleil   in the sun
à l'ombre   in the shade
à l'étranger   abroad

DOSSIER 7

AU TRAVAIL

READING COMPREHENSION

1

> Le travail, c'est la santé,
> Rien faire, c'est la conserver:
> Les prisonniers du boulot
> Font pas de vieux os.
>
> (Refrain of popular French song)

a According to the song, what must you do to keep your health?
b What is said about the 'prisoners of work'?

2

NOS SAPEURS-POMPIERS DANS LE FEU DE L'ACTION
Les sapeurs-pompiers de notre ville ont procédé aux interventions suivantes durant la semaine du 12 au 18 août.
Jeudi 12: 6h30 secours d'une personne rue du Tivoli; 16h05 ouverture d'une porte rue de la Mairie.
Vendredi 13: 8h30 accident de mobylette, blessé transporté clinique.
Samedi 14: fausse alerte
Dimanche 15; 10h30 accident de la route, un blessé transporté clinique; 17h00 feu de maison à Villedieu.
Lundi 16: 18h00 destruction d'un essaim de guêpes.
Mardi 17: 7h00 destruction d'un essaim de guêpes; 10h15 sauvetage d'un chat sur un toit.
Mercredi: 7h10 destruction d'un essaim de guêpes; 13h00 feu de maison à Loupia; 18h30 accident de la route, un blessé transporté clinique.

a What were the firemen called to do on Thursday afternoon?
b On which two days were they called to a fire?
c What did they do on Tuesday 17th at 10.15 a.m.
d On which day was there a hoax call?
e On which days did they deal with swarms of wasps?
f How many street accidents did they attend, and on which days?

3

EMPLOIS Demandes
Prends tous travaux jardin. Tél. 65-86-28
JF 20 ans cherche heures ménage ou demi service Tél. 65-32-30 de 16h à 20h.
Infirmière cherche poste dans maison enfants. Tél. 72-16-30
Secrétaire médicale 25 ans, bonne culture générale, cherche emploi plein temps sur Montpellier et environs, libre 01-09 Ecrire Havas, Montpellier 198, 785
JH 22 ans, possédant diplôme construction, cherche emploi stable sur Montpellier et région. Tél. 75-24-49
Suédoise, 19 ans, cherche place au pair. Tél. 60-40-11.

a What type of job is the nurse seeking?
b i Does the medical secretary want full or part-time work?
  ii When is she free to begin work?
c What nationality is the girl looking for an au pair job?
d What number would you telephone if you wanted some gardening done?
e i What type of work is the twenty year old girl looking for?
  ii At what time can you telephone her?
f i What sort of qualification does the young man of twenty-two have?
  ii What type of work is he seeking?

4

EMPLOIS Offres
Recherchons pour Arles, vendeuse vêtements qualifiée. âge maxi. 30 ans. Ecrire avec références à Havas Arles 60,000
Demandons personne confiance pour garde enfant. Madame Michel Tél. 80-00-58.
Magasin de sport Nîmes, cherche vendeur débutant, de préférence ancien sportif. Ecrire, avec photo, à Havas Montpellier 13,822
Urgent – hôtel recherche un réceptionniste de nuit. Anglais exigé. Tel. 241-44-88
Urgent – recherche pour Aix-en-Provence jeune employée de maison ayant permis conduire. Références exigées. Tel. 82-54-07.
Cherche secretaire bilingue anglais, 25 ans environ, contrat longue durée, mi-temps. Tel. 735-35-33

a What type of person is wanted as a child's nurse?
b i What type of shop is looking for a sales assistant without experience?
  ii What must you do to apply for this job?
c What type of sales assistant is wanted in Arles? Give **two** points.
d If you want the hotel receptionist's job, what must you be able to do?
e If you take the bilingual secretary's job:
  i Would you work full or part-time?
  ii What advantage does the job have?
f i What sort of job is available in Aix-en-Provence?
  ii Which two things must you have for this job?

5

The following passage is taken from the novel *325 000 francs* by Roger Vailland. The central character, Busard, is engaged to Marie-Jeanne, and they plan to marry when he has earned enough to put down the deposit on a snack-bar in the country which they want to buy. The sum needed is 325 000 francs. Busard is working in a factory which makes plastic toys. A heavy machine stamps the toy shape onto melted plastic. Busard must cut the plastic thread, remove the toy and throw it into a container – every twelve seconds, during an eight-hour shift. He is paid piece rates, so, in order to produce more, he works with the safety device (la grille) raised. It is his final night shift, and he is desperately tired . . .

◀ Busard travaillait maintenant grille levée.
Il trancha, sépara, jeta.
Le petit temps gagné, à ne pas lever et baisser la grille, lui fit le même effet que quand on pose un fardeau. Il était plus léger, il respirait mieux.
Mais il pensait:
‹Je dois arrêter la presse et remettre la grille.›
Il sentait cela très vivement. Il savait tout du danger de travailler sans dispositif de sécurité. Rien qu'à y penser il sentait dans sa main le poids de la machine qui se referme. Mais il se dit aussi:
‹Si je replace la grille, je perds plus d'une minute, j'ai l'amende, et je n'aurai pas fini demain à huit heures.›
C'était absurde, qu'il finît le travail demain ou après-demain – qu'est-ce que ça pourrait faire? Il les aurait, ses 325 000 francs. Mais il n'avait plus l'esprit clair, tout se brouillait dans sa tête.
Il trancha, sépara, jeta.
‹Je vais me faire pincer les doigts. Je ne dois pas me faire pincer les doigts.›
Il regarda l'horloge. Deux heures.
Il mit une extrême attention dans son travail. La machine restait ouverte dix secondes. La main ne restait engagée dans la machine que quatre secondes.
Il essaya de retirer la main chaque fois le plus vite possible. De cette façon, c'était plus sûr.
Il compta à haute voix le temps que la main demeurait dans la machine. Quatre secondes et demie.
Il pensa: ‹Je vais me faire pincer les doigts.›
Il regarda l'horloge. Deux heures dix.

Il compta. Sa main resta presque six secondes dans la machine.
Il pensa: ‹C'est absolument sûr que je vais me faire pincer les doigts.›
Il décida: ‹Je vais replacer la grille . . .›
Il poussa un cri. L'ouvrier à côté se trouva tout de suite près de lui. La main était engagée jusqu'au poignet dans la machine fermée – une pression de plusieurs milliers de kilos. Busard perdit connaissance.
Les autres ouvriers accouraient. L'un d'eux était déjà au téléphone. Bientôt après, l'ambulance arriva. Les autres ouvriers retournèrent à leurs presses. ▶

Answer in English the following questions:
a What **three** movements must Busard perform?
b In what ways did he feel better working without the safety device? (**two** things)
c Explain exactly what the consequences would be if he stopped in order to put back the safety device.
d What is the time when he first looks at the clock?
e For how long did the machine stay open?
f How did he try to make certain that he was safe?
g What did he do to check how long he was taking each time?
h Describe the exact sequence of events from the moment of the accident.

Translate from the beginning of the passage down to '. . . demain à huit heures.'

LISTENING COMPREHENSION

1

Listen carefully to the passage before answering in English the following questions:
a   What is Marc Giraud's occupation?
b   At what age did he leave school?
c   How long has he been working for 'La Dépêche'?
d   Which **two** topics does he write about?
e   What did he report on last summer?
f   Why did he enjoy this assignment?
g   On which subject is he now doing a series of articles?
h   When did he write an article on Jacques Danot?
i   What does Jacques want to become?
j   On which days does Jacques work in Lille?
k   Why is Jacques lucky?
l   How old is Chantal Lenoir?
m   How many days a week does she study?
n   At what type of college does she study?
o   Which day does she find particularly tiring?
p   At what time does she finish work on Saturdays?

2

You are going to hear an interview which was broadcast on French radio in a series about young people and their holiday jobs. Listen carefully before attempting the following exercises.

Read the following statements about the passage you have just heard, and write 'vrai' or 'faux' for each one.
a   Bernard est un jeune Français.
b   Pendant les vacances il travaille dans un camping.
c   Le matin, il a deux heures de libre.
d   Il aime nager et jouer au tennis.
e   Le soir, il fait la plonge, mais il ne sert pas les clients.
f   Il ne travaille pas après onze heures.
g   Il gagne bien, mais il doit payer ses repas.
h   Les campeurs sont gentils.
i   A Argelès, en été, il fait beau, il y a du soleil.
j   Bernard est content à Argelès.

Answer in English the following questions:
a   What age is Bernard?
b   What nationality is he?
c   At what time does he get up?
d   State one job that he does during the morning.
e   When is he free?
f   What **two** things does he do in his free time?
g   State one thing the boss may ask him to do in the evenings.
h   At what time does he finish work?
i   How much does he earn?
j   Name **two** things which, according to Bernard, are his 'real' wages.

96

GRAMMAR EXERCISES

1

Translate these sentences into French:
a The old men were sitting in the sun.
b She looked at us in a strange way.
c We have been living in France for two years.
d I am washing the car for my father.
e It rained for two hours and then the sun began to shine.
f They left at eight o'clock in the evening.
g Madame Durand lives in Provence.
h Monsieur Boisvert spent his holiday in Portugal.
i They have bought a house in the country.
j We are going to France in June.

2

Copy the following story, filling in the gaps. Note that in some cases the gap is part of a word, in others it is a whole word.

« Evelyne Duval avait dix-neuf ans. Elle était secrétaire. Lundi matin, elle s'est l—— à sept heures et demie. Après —— pris le petit déjeuner, elle a qu—— la maison à huit heures et quart.

Arr—— au bureau, elle a dit bonjour à Nicole, la réceptionniste, et puis elle a commencé —— ouvrir le courrier. A dix heures, son patron, Monsieur Lambert, —— a demandé de venir dans son bureau, car il voulait —— dicter des lettres. Evelyne n'aimait pas beaucoup cela, mais —— fallait bien le faire.

Pendant l'après-midi, Evelyne a tapé les lettres —— la machine. A cinq heures, Monsieur Lambert a signé les lettres, et il a dit —— Evelyne —— les mettre tout de suite —— la poste. Puis, il a ajouté: ‹Vous savez, Mademoiselle Duval, je —— très content —— votre travail. Donc, j'ai l'intention —— augmenter votre salaire dès le début —— mois prochain.›
‹Merci beaucoup, monsieur,› a r—— Evelyne. Elle a tout de suite téléphoné —— son ami Paul —— lui dire la bonne nouvelle.
‹Fantastique! Il faut fêter ça!› a c—— Paul. ‹Je t'invite —— dîner ce soir —— restaurant. D'accord?›
‹Oui, merci,› a d—— Evelyne, ‹Je t'attendrai —— moi à sept heures et demie. A tout —— l'heure.› »

3

This exercise should be done after exercise 2 has been completed and corrected.
Answer in French these questions on the previous passage:
a Quel âge avait Evelyne?
b Quel était son métier?
c Qu'est-ce qu'elle a fait en arrivant au bureau? (deux choses)
d Qu'est-ce que Monsieur Lambert a demandé à Evelyne de faire à dix heures?
e A quelle heure Monsieur Lambert a-t-il signé les lettres?
f Puis qu'est-ce qu'il a dit à Evelyne de faire?
g Quelle bonne nouvelle a-t-il donnée à Evelyne?
h Pourquoi Evelyne a-t-elle téléphoné à Paul?
i Qu'est-ce que Paul l'a invitée à faire?
j Où allaient-ils se retrouver?

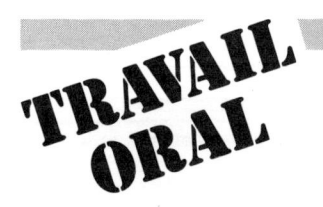

TRAVAIL ORAL

1

You are being interviewed by Madame Marceau, who wants an English 'au pair' to help look after her two young children.

MADAME MARCEAU	Bonjour mademoiselle. Comment vous appelez-vous?
VOUS	(*Give your name.*)
MADAME M	Et quel âge avez-vous?
VOUS	(*Give your age.*)
MADAME M	Et où habitez-vous?
VOUS	(*Say what town you live in.*)
MADAME M	Pourquoi cherchez-vous un emploi au pair?

VOUS	(*Say that you would like the opportunity to speak French, and you like children.*)
MADAME M	Vous êtes habituée aux jeunes enfants?
VOUS	(*Say yes, your married sister has two small children.*)
MADAME M	Merci, mademoiselle, je vais vous écrire d'ici quelques jours.
VOUS	(*Thank her politely and say goodbye.*)

2

You are being interviewed for a holiday job by Alain Bontemps, who runs a 'colonie de vacances' (holiday centre for children) in the Pyrenees.

ALAIN	Bonjour. Comment t'appelles-tu?
VOUS	(*Give your name.*)
ALAIN	Et tu as quel âge?
VOUS	(*Give your age.*)
ALAIN	Pourquoi veux-tu venir travailler dans le Midi?
VOUS	(*Say you would like to go to France in the summer, but you can't afford a holiday.*)
ALAIN	Tu es sportif?
VOUS	(*Say yes, and mention two or three sports that you enjoy.*)
ALAIN	Tu as déjà travaillé dans une colonie de vacances?
VOUS	(*Say no, but you work in a youth club.*)
ALAIN	Bon. Je crois que j'aurai une place pour toi. Je vais t'écrire bientôt.
VOUS	(*Thank him and say goodbye.*)

3

Ask three questions about the 'au pair' job, and three more about the holiday centre job, for example: when can you begin; what hours must you work; how much will you be paid; what free time you will have; whether you will have your own room.

4

Prepare a short talk (one minute) in French about any Saturday job, holiday job, or voluntary work you do, or have done.

TRAVAIL ECRIT

1

Write a story based on the following summary:

Alain Delage, dix-sept ans – premier jour au travail dans un magasin – se lève de bonne heure – manque l'autobus – obligé de prendre taxi – arrive juste à l'heure.

Write the story using **past** tenses. (*120 words*)

2

> Urgent – cherche serveur/serveuse pour café-bar, juillet, août.
> Ecrire Monsieur J. Dore, Café des Sports, Canet.

Write a reply to the above advertisement. Give your age, say that you speak French fairly well, and have worked in a café. Say when you could begin work. Ask how much you would be paid and what hours you would have to work.

(*100/120 words*)

3 Write a story which the pictures suggest to you.
Remember to use **past** tenses. (*120 words*)

VOCABULARY

Reading comprehension

1
boulot (*m*) – work (slang)
conserver – to keep
os (*m*) – bone
santé (*f*) – health

2
essaim (*m*) – swarm
faux (*m*), fausse (*f*) – false
guêpe (*f*) – wasp
ouverture (*f*) – opening
sapeur-pompier (*m*) – fireman
secours (*m*) – help
toit (*m*) – roof

3
environs (*m pl*) – surroundings, surrounding area
infirmière (*f*) – nurse
libre – free
ménage (*m*) – housework

4
contrat (*m*) – contract
débutant(e) – beginner
environ – about
exigé – required, demanded
permis (*m*) de conduire – driving licence
vendeur (*m*) – salesman
vendeuse (*f*) – saleslady

5
amende (*f*) – fine
arrêter – to stop
baisser – to lower
se brouiller – to be confused, jumbled
clair – clear
compter – to count
dispositif (*m*) de sécurité – safety device
doigt (*m*) – finger
esprit (*m*) – mind
fardeau (*m*) – burden
gagné – gained
horloge (*f*) – clock
jeter – to throw
léger – light
lever – to raise
même – same
mieux – better
perdre – to lose
poids (*m*) – weight
poignet (*m*) – wrist
poser – to put down, place
pousser un cri – to utter a cry
respirer – to breathe
retirer – to withdraw
sentir – to feel
trancher – to cut
vivement – keenly

Listening comprehension

1
apprentissage (*m*) – apprenticeship
avoir l'occasion – to have an opportunity
célèbre – famous
coiffure (*f*) – hairdressing
course (*f*) – race
emploi (*m*) – job
jusqu'à – until
partout – everywhere
série (*f*) – series

2
émission (*f*) – broadcast
faire la plonge – to do the washing up (in a café, etc.)
gratuit – free of charge
Midi (*m*) – the south of France
nettoyage (*m*) – cleaning
poubelle (*f*) – dustbin
pourboire (*m*) – tip
ramasser – to pick up, to collect
repas (*m*) – meal
salaire (*m*) – wages
salle (*f*) de jeux – games room
verre (*m*) – glass
vider – to empty
vrai – true, real

GRAMMAR

1

Verbs followed by an infinitive

In this section we are dealing with verbs which are followed by an infinitive without any preposition.
These verbs can be divided into several groups:

> Verbs of motion:
> aller – to go
> courir – to run
> descendre – to go down
> entrer – to go in
> monter – to go up
> retourner – to go back
> venir – to come

EXAMPLE:
Je suis venu voir ta nouvelle voiture.
I have come to see your new car.

Il est retourné chercher son parapluie.
He went back to look for his umbrella.

2
> Verbs of hearing, seeing, etc:
> entendre – to hear
> regarder – to watch, to look at
> sembler – to seem
> sentir – to feel
> voir – to see

EXAMPLE:
Je l'ai entendu crier.
I heard him shouting.

3
> Verbs of thinking, etc:
> aimer – to like
> croire – to think, to believe
> désirer – to want
> oser – to dare
> penser – to think
> préférer – to prefer

EXAMPLE:
Je préfère rester a la maison.
I prefer to stay at home.

Il n'a pas osé parler.
He did not dare to speak.

4
> Verbs meaning can, must, want, etc.:
> devoir – must
> pouvoir – to be able, can
> savoir – to know (how to . . .)
> vouloir – to want

EXAMPLE:
Je dois partir tout de suite.
I must leave at once.

● NOTE the difference in meaning of 'savoir' and 'pouvoir'.

It is shown in the following conversation:
‹Est-ce que tu sais jouer au tennis?›
‹Oui. Mais je ne peux pas jouer aujourd'hui; j'ai mal à la jambe.›

'Can you (do you know how to) play tennis?'
'Yes. But I can't (am unable to) play today; I have hurt my leg.'

Verbs of communication

Most verbs which deal with communicating are followed by 'à', i.e. they take an indirect object.

This list should be learnt by heart:

> *crier – to shout
> écrire – to write
> pardonner – to forgive
> parler – to talk, to speak
> *promettre – to promise
> répondre – to reply, to answer
> téléphoner – to telephone
> *conseiller – to advise
> *défendre – to forbid
> *demander – to ask
> *dire – to tell
> *ordonner – to order
> *permettre – to permit, to allow

EXAMPLE:
J'ai téléphoné au docteur.   I telephoned the doctor.
Je lui ai téléphoné.   I telephoned him.

The verbs marked * in the above list take 'à' before the person and 'de' before the following infinitive.
EXAMPLE:
demander **à** quelqu'un **de** faire quelque chose
to ask someone to do something
EXAMPLE:
J'ai demandé au docteur de venir tout de suite.
I asked the doctor to come at once.

Je lui ai demandé de venir tout de suite.
I asked him to come at once.

La mère a defendu à ses enfants de jouer dans la rue.
The mother forbade her children to play in the street.

Translating 'in'

1. Usually **'dans'**
   dans une boîte — in a box
   assis dans un fauteuil — sitting in an armchair

2. **'En'**
   en colère — in anger, in a temper
   en paix — in peace
   en ville — in (the) town
   en juin — in June
   en hiver — in winter
   en été — in summer
   en automne — in autumn
   en 1945 — in 1945

3. **'De'**
   de mauvaise humeur — in a bad mood
   de bonne humeur — in a good mood
   de cette façon } in this (that) way
   de cette manière }
   vêtu de — dressed in
   habillé de — dressed in
   une heure de l'après-midi — one o'clock in the afternoon

4. **'À'**
   à la campagne — in the country
   au printemps — in the spring
   aux champs — in the fields
   au soleil — in the sun
   à l'ombre — in the shade
   à mon avis — in my opinion
   au seizième siècle — in the sixteenth century
   au mois de juin — in the month of June

5. **Not translated**
   le matin — in the morning
   l'après-midi — in the afternoon

Translating 'for'

1. **'Car'** – used to join two parts of a sentence, i.e. when 'for' means 'because'.
   EXAMPLE:
   Je me suis dépêché, car mon père n'aime pas que je rentre tard.
   I hurried, for my father doesn't like me to get home late.

2. **'Pour'** – when 'for' is a preposition.
   EXAMPLE:
   J'ai acheté un cadeau pour ma mère.
   I bought a present for my mother.

   Je ne comprends pas ce livre, il est trop difficile pour moi.
   I don't understand that book, it's too difficult for me.

3. In time expressions:
   a **'Pendant'** – referring to an action completed in the past.
   EXAMPLE:
   Il a demeuré à Paris pendant six mois.
   He lived in Paris for six months (*but he no longer lives there*).

   b **'Depuis'** – referring to a continuing action.
   EXAMPLE:
   J'apprends le français depuis quatre ans.
   I have been learning French for four years (*and I am still learning, therefore, present tense*).

   Elle travaillait à Londres depuis deux ans.
   She had been working in London for two years (*and she was still working there*, so imperfect tense).

   c **'Pour'** – referring to future plans.
   EXAMPLE:
   Je vais partir en Espagne pour quinze jours.
   I am going off to Spain for a fortnight.

4. **Other expressions with 'for'**
   sauter de joie — to jump for joy
   se marier par amour — to marry for love
   remercier de — to thank (someone) for

   ● REMEMBER:
   attendre — to wait for (do **not** translate 'for')
   J'attendais l'autobus — I was waiting for the bus.
   BUT:
   J'ai attendu pendant une demi-heure.
   I waited for half an hour.

DOSSIER 8

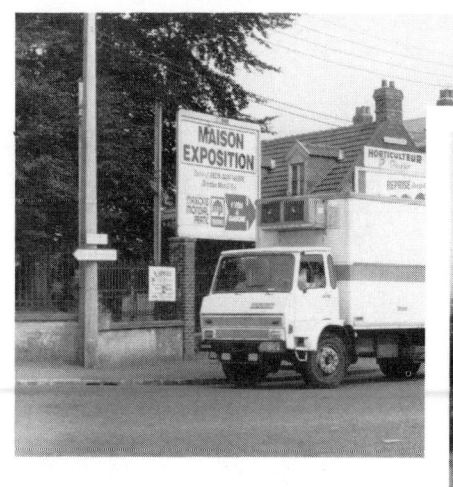

ON ROULE!

READING COMPREHENSION

Read these extracts from newspapers and answer the questions in English.

1

Vers 11h. mardi sur la Route Nationale 34 près de Charenton, une camionnette conduite par M. Jules Lairy a percuté un cycliste.
La camionnette, qui venait de Nogent, tournait à gauche pour aller vers Charenton.
Gravement blessé, le cycliste, M. Louis Blaise, 55 ans, a été hospitalisé à Rennes.

a Did the accident occur on a main or minor road?
b Which **two** vehicles were involved?
c What was the condition of the cyclist?

2

Vendredi, vers 8h. 20, près de Montgermont, un automobiliste, M. Jean-Luc Renault, commerçant de Rennes, a perdu le contrôle de son véhicule et est allé heurter un pylone électrique en bordure de la route.
Conséquence du choc extrêmement violent: Le conducteur du véhicule a été tué sur le coup.

a What was the job of the car driver?
b How many vehicles were involved in the accident?
c Why did the accident happen?
d Where was the electric pylon?
e What was the result of the accident?

3

BOUCLEZ VOTRE CEINTURE! C'EST PLUS SÛR!

a What are you being told to do?
b Why?

4

UNE 'PREMIERE' POUR MICHELE MOUTON

En gagnant samedi 10 octobre le 23me Rallye de San-Remo, la Française, Michèle Mouton et sa coéquipière italienne Fabrizia Pons ont signé un succès doublement historique. C'est en effet la première fois qu'un équipage féminin gagne une manche du championnat du monde des rallyes depuis sa création en 1973.
C'est aussi le premier succès d'une Audi Quattro dans une épreuve comptant pour le championnat du monde.

a What type of event has Michèle Mouton just won?
b Who is Fabrizia Pons?
c In what two respects is this victory a 'first'?

5

Ville d'Angoulême

CIRCULATION

ARRETONS

Par ordre de la Feldkommandantur, la population d'Angoulême est informée que la circulation des piétons doit se faire sur les trottoirs du côté droit, dans le sens de la marche.
Toute personne qui ne se conformera pas à cette réglementation sera l'objet d'un procès-verbal.

Le maire
GUILLON

Cette affiche fut apposée le 31 août, 1940 sur les murs de la ville d'Angoulême en France, pendant l'occupation allemande.

a To which group of people is the order addressed?
b What are they ordered to do?

6

a Name the **four** types of driving offence quoted in the police report.
b When did this report appear?
c How long is the government giving motorists to improve the situation?
d What will happen if the situation does not improve?
e Which **two** aspects of driving are going to be watched particularly closely?
f Why is the second of these so important?

> ‹Feux rouges brûlés ... Ceinture non bouclée ... conduite sous l'emprise de l'alcool ... limitations de vitesse négligées ... les automobilistes respectent de moins en moins les règles élémentaires du code de la route ...› selon un rapport de la Gendarmerie Nationale, publié il y a quelques jours.
>
> A la suite de ce rapport, le gouvernement a averti les conducteurs que si, au terme des six mois à venir, la situation ne s'est pa améliorée, les limitations de vitesses pourraient être abaissées.
>
> Deux aspects de la conduite vont être particulièrement surveillés; les conditions de dépassement, et les distances de sécurité entre véhicules, principale cause d'accident sur l'autoroute.

7

PARTEZ SANS PAYER AVEC VOTRE NISSAN CHERRY 1.5 TURBO

APPORT PERSONNEL NEANT
Du 16 novembre au
16 décembre 1985

42.534 F

Traction avant
Boîte 5 vitesses
5 portes
Vitres teintées
Peinture métallisée
Pare-brise feuilleté
Autoradio de série

avec carte grise et vignette
Garantie deux ans – Pièces et main – d'œuvre
DATSUN assistance un an

DATSUN: LA PLUS BELLE INVENTION DEPUIS L'AUTOMOBILE

a What is especially attractive about paying for this car?
b How many gears does the car have?
c What are you told about its windows?
d For how long is it guaranteed?
e What does the guarantee cover?

8

Les conduites en état d'ivresse

● M Pattrick Le Vourch, 23 ans, demeurant à Kerverven, en Brignogan-Plages

Trois mois de suspension de permis, 1.000F d'amende.

● M. Roland Cosques, 24 ans, préposé des P.T.T. demeurant 6, rue de Bohars, à Gullers.

Huit mois de suspension de permis, 2.000F d'amende.

a What crime have both these people committed?
b For how long has M. Roland Cosquer lost his licence?
c How much has M. Patrick Le Vourch been fined?

9

The following is an extract from *Encore du Nicolas*, one of a series of books which is very popular with French children.
The headmaster has received complaints about the way in which Nicolas and the other pupils cross the road to school. The children have therefore been given instruction in the Highway Code . . .

Le directeur est entré.
— Debout! a dit la maîtresse.
— Assis! a dit le directeur. Eh bien! mademoiselle, vous avez fait la leçon de Code à vos élèves?
— Oui, Monsieur le Directeur, a dit la maîtresse. Ils ont été très sages, et je suis sûre qu'ils ont très bien compris.
Alors le directeur a fait un grand sourire et il a dit:
— Très bien. Parfait! J'espère que je n'aurai plus de plaintes de la police au sujet de la conduite de mes élèves. Enfin, nous verrons tout ça dans la pratique.
Le directeur est sorti; nous nous sommes rassis, et puis la cloche a sonné; nous nous sommes levés pour sortir, mais la maîtresse nous a dit:
— Pas si vite, pas si vite! Vous allez descendre gentiment, et je veux vous voir traverser la rue. Nous verrons si vous avez compris la leçon.
Nous sommes sortis de l'école avec la maîtresse, et l'agent de police a fait un sourire quand il nous a vus. Il a arrêté les autos, et il nous a fait signe de passer.
— Allez-y les enfants, nous a dit la maîtresse. Et sans courir! Je vous observe d'ici.
Alors, nous avons traversé la rue, tout doucement, les uns derrière les autres, et quand nous sommes arrivés de l'autre côté, nous avons vu la maîtresse qui parlait avec l'agent de police, sur le trottoir, en riant, et le directeur qui nous regardait de la fenêtre de son bureau.
— Très bien! nous a crié la maîtresse. M. l'Agent et moi sommes très contents de vous. A demain, les enfants!
Alors nous avons tous retraversé la rue en courant pour lui donner la main.

Answer in English the following questions:
a What hope does the headmaster express?
b How would you translate 'Enfin on verra tout ça dans la pratique.'?
c What **three** things did the policeman do on seeing the children?
d What was the teacher doing while the children crossed the road?
e What was the headmaster doing?
f Which particular sentence makes this into a humorous incident?
g Explain your answer.

Answer in French the following questions:
a Qu'est-ce que le directeur a demandé à la maîtresse? (Ne donnez pas ses mot exacts.)
b Qu'est-ce que le directeur espère ne plus recevoir?
c Qu'est-ce que les enfants ont fait quand la cloche a sonné?
d Puis qu'est-ce que la maîtresse a dit aux enfants? (Ne donnez pas ses mot exacts.)
e Comment les enfants ont-ils traversé la rue la première fois?
f Pourquoi ont-ils retraversé la rue en courant?

Translate into English from the beginning of the passage down to '. . . compris la leçon.'

106

LISTENING COMPREHENSION

1

A la station-service

Listen carefully to the passage before answering in English the following questions:

a How much and what type of petrol does Madame Petit want?
b When will Madame Petit's husband join them on holiday?
c What sort of property do they have in the Dordogne?
d How long did it take them to cross Limoges last year?
e What **two** reasons does Madame Petit give for this?
f Why, according to the garage attendant, will it be easier this year?
g What does she ask the garage attendant to do?
h What unfortunate event had occurred as they left Poitiers?
i What does the garage attendant also do?
j How much does he charge Madame Petit?

2

Tourists in the Sahara Desert

Listen carefully to the passage before answering in English the following questions:

a Why did the French tourists put out a distress call?
b By whom was it heard?
c How many cars did the expedition have, and what was their condition?
d What was the first step taken by the French police?
e How did they do this?
f What did the Minister for External Affairs do?
g What did the Algerian police confirm on Monday?
h In what condition were the tourists?
i Why had the tourists been trapped in their cars?
j What sort of action did the Algerian police take?
k What did a spokesman for the French embassy say?

GRAMMAR EXERCISES

1

Translate these sentences into French:
a The house was surrounded by a wall.
b This room is seven metres long by five metres wide.
c I shall arrive before three o'clock.
d By working hard you will succeed.
e You must learn this poem by heart.
f I must finish my work before he returns.
g The teacher was standing in front of the class.
h We went to see a play by Molière.

107

2 Write out the following text, choosing the correct item from each box.

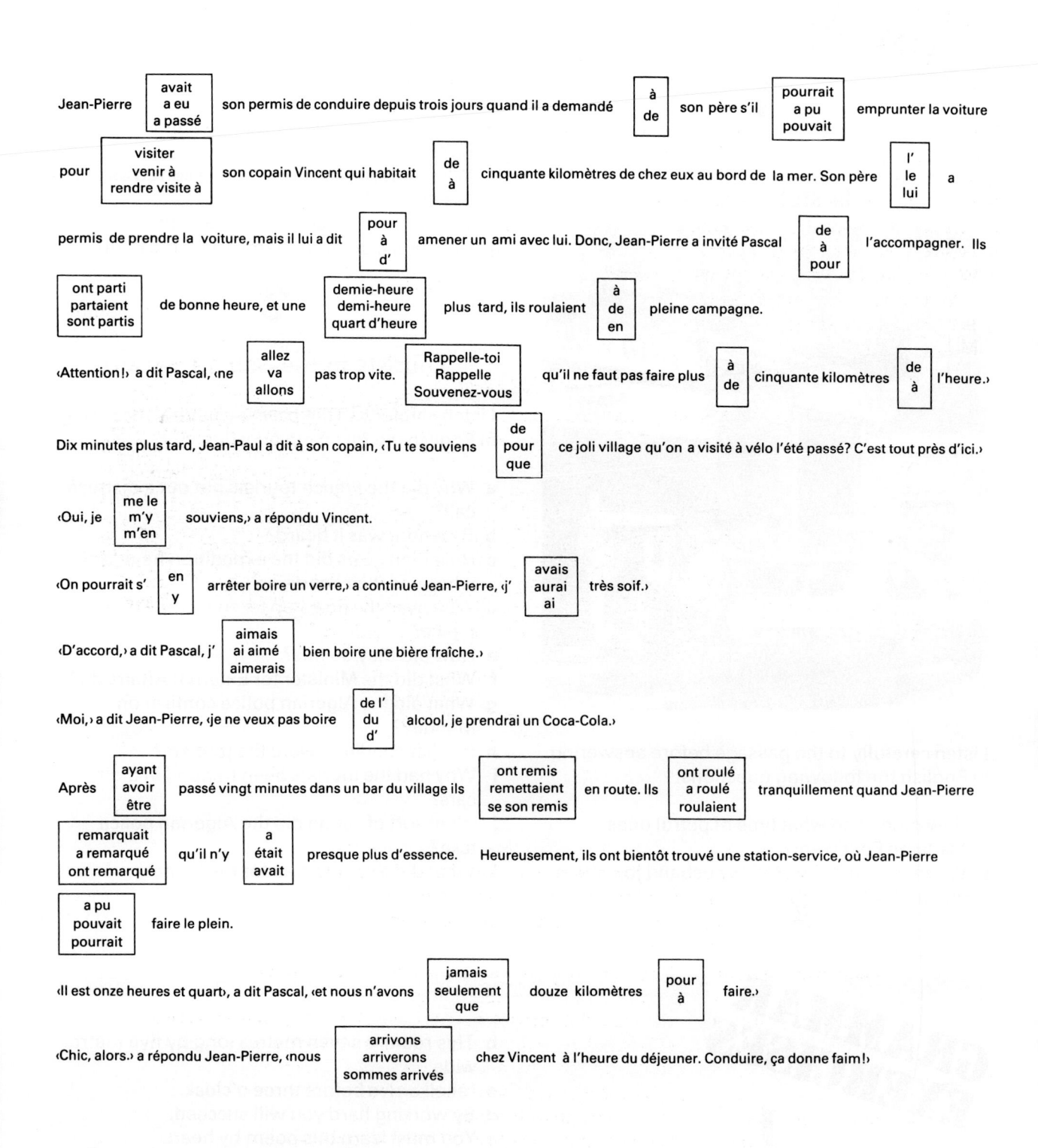

Jean-Pierre [avait / a eu / a passé] son permis de conduire depuis trois jours quand il a demandé [à / de] son père s'il [pourrait / a pu / pouvait] emprunter la voiture pour [visiter / venir à / rendre visite à] son copain Vincent qui habitait [de / à] cinquante kilomètres de chez eux au bord de la mer. Son père [l' / le / lui] a permis de prendre la voiture, mais il lui a dit [pour / à / d'] amener un ami avec lui. Donc, Jean-Pierre a invité Pascal [de / à / pour] l'accompagner. Ils [ont parti / partaient / sont partis] de bonne heure, et une [demie-heure / demi-heure / quart d'heure] plus tard, ils roulaient [à / de / en] pleine campagne.

«Attention!» a dit Pascal, «ne [allez / va / allons] pas trop vite. [Rappelle-toi / Rappelle / Souvenez-vous] qu'il ne faut pas faire plus [à / de] cinquante kilomètres [de / à] l'heure.»

Dix minutes plus tard, Jean-Paul a dit à son copain, «Tu te souviens [de / pour / que] ce joli village qu'on a visité à vélo l'été passé? C'est tout près d'ici.»

«Oui, je [me le / m'y / m'en] souviens,» a répondu Vincent.

«On pourrait s'[en / y] arrêter boire un verre,» a continué Jean-Pierre, «j'[avais / aurai / ai] très soif.»

«D'accord,» a dit Pascal, j'[aimais / ai aimé / aimerais] bien boire une bière fraîche.»

«Moi,» a dit Jean-Pierre, «je ne veux pas boire [de l' / du / d'] alcool, je prendrai un Coca-Cola.»

Après [ayant / avoir / être] passé vingt minutes dans un bar du village ils [ont remis / remettaient / se son remis] en route. Ils [ont roulé / a roulé / roulaient] tranquillement quand Jean-Pierre [remarquait / a remarqué / ont remarqué] qu'il n'y [a / était / avait] presque plus d'essence. Heureusement, ils ont bientôt trouvé une station-service, où Jean-Pierre [a pu / pouvait / pourrait] faire le plein.

«Il est onze heures et quart», a dit Pascal, «et nous n'avons [jamais / seulement / que] douze kilomètres [pour / à] faire.»

«Chic, alors.» a répondu Jean-Pierre, «nous [arrivons / arriverons / sommes arrivés] chez Vincent à l'heure du déjeuner. Conduire, ça donne faim!»

108

TRAVAIL ORAL

1

Refer to the photograph of the car and to the vocabulary at the end of the dossier to prepare these oral tasks.

You have stopped at a garage while motoring in France. Make these requests in French:
a Fill up the car, please.
b Forty litres of four-star petrol please.
c Would you check the brakes please?
d Would you check the oil please?
e Would you clean the windscreen please?
f Is there a ring road at Bordeaux?
g Is there a lot of traffic in the centre of Montauban?

le volant, le rétroviseur, le coffre, le pare-brise, l'essuie-glace, le phare, les pneus

2

You are travelling by car in France and have a puncture. A friendly French motorist stops and offers to help. Fill in your part of the conversation. (You are given instructions in brackets.)

CHAUFFEUR FRANÇAIS	Bonjour. Il y a quelque chose qui ne ne va pas?
VOUS	(*Yes. You've got a puncture.*)
CHAUFFEUR FRANÇAIS	Oh, quel dommage! Je vais vous aider. Vous avez un cric?
VOUS	(*It's very kind of him. Yes, you've got a jack. It's in the boot.*)
CHAUFFEUR FRANÇAIS	Voilà. Ce sera vite fait. Et la roue de secours?
VOUS	(*The spare wheel is in the boot too.*)
CHAUFFEUR FRANÇAIS	Vous avez un tournevis?
VOUS	(*You're sorry, you haven't got a screwdriver.*)
CHAUFFEUR FRANÇAIS	Ça ne fait rien. J'en ai un dans la voiture. Voilà, c'est fini.
VOUS	(*Thank him, and offer him some tissues to clean his hands.*)
CHAUFFEUR FRANÇAIS	Merci. Au revoir. Bonnes vacances et bonne route!

3

You have witnessed a minor accident on a busy French road. Answer the policeman's questions. You are given guidelines in brackets.

AGENT   Votre nom, monsieur/mademoiselle?
VOUS   (Give your name, spell our your surname.)
AGENT   Vous êtes en vacances?
VOUS   (Yes, you're here on holiday for a fortnight.)
AGENT   Quelle est votre adresse ici?
VOUS   (Hôtel Beauséjour, Place Jean Jaurès, Collioure.)
AGENT   Qu'est-ce que vous avez vu?
VOUS   (You saw a blue Peugeot and a red Renault. They collided, but no one was hurt.)
AGENT   Est-ce que la Peugeot roulait vite?
VOUS   (Yes, it was travelling rather fast for such a busy road.)
AGENT   Et la Renault rouge?
VOUS   (It was coming from the street on the right. It was travelling quite slowly, about thirty kilometres an hour.)
AGENT   Vous avez autre chose à me dire?
VOUS   (You think it was the fault of the Peugeot driver. He was going too fast, and he didn't observe the priority of traffic from the right.)
AGENT   Merci, monsieur/mademoiselle.

TRAVAIL ECRIT

1

Voici une page du carnet de l'agent de police Jean Duvivier où il a noté les détails d'un accident qui s'est passé hier matin quand il était de service.
En vous servant de ces détails écrivez le rapport qu'il doit faire à Monsieur l'Inspecteur.

(150 words)

Endroit – carrefour Rue des Princes et Avenue Charles de Gaulle

Heure – 07.16 matin
Date – jeudi 20 juin
Véhicules – poids-lourd
            2CV rouge
            vélo

Feux rouges ne fonctionnaient pas
Cycliste légèrement blessé genou et tête transp. hôpital
2CV – phare gauche brisé
Poids-lourd – indmne

2

Refer to exercise 3 in the TRAVAIL ORAL section and write an account of the incident.

3

Write a story which the following pictures suggest to you.

VOCABULARY

Reading comprehension

1
blessé – wounded, injured
camionnette (f) – van
conduit – driven
percuter – to hit, crash into

2
(en) bordure de – beside
commerçant (m) – shopkeeper
perdre – to lose
sur le coup – instantly
tuer – to kill

3
boucler – to buckle, fasten
ceinture (f) – belt

4
épreuve (f) – test
gagner – to win
manche (f) – (here) a 'leg', i.e. section of a race or competition

5
affiche (f) – poster
mur (m) – wall

6
abaisser – to lower
s'améliorer – to get better
avertir – to warn
brûler les feux – to go through
  rouges   traffic lights
code (m) de la – highway code
  route
conduite (f) – driving
de moins en moins – less and less
dépassement (m) – overtaking
limitation (f)
  de vitesse – speed limit
rapport (m) – report
règle (f) – rule
selon – according to
surveiller – to watch, supervise
(au) terme de – at the end of

7
pièce (f) de
  rechange – spare part
vitesse (f) – gear

8
amende (f) – fine
ivresse – drunkenness
permis (m) – driving licence
  (de conduire)

9
cloche (f) – bell
conduite (f) – behaviour
directeur (m) – headmaster
plainte (f) – complaint
sage – sensible, well-behaved
sonner – to ring
traverser – to cross
trottoir (m) – pavement

Listening comprehension

1
bonne route! – have a safe journey! (to someone travelling by car)
boulevard (m)
  périphérique – ring road
campagne (f) – country
chance (f) – (good) luck
circulation (f) – traffic
conduire – to drive
étranger (m) – foreigner
étranger (m) – foreign
  étrangère (f)
gentil – kind
je vous dois – how much do
  combien? I owe you?
nettoyer – to clean
pare-brise (m) – windscreen
pénible – difficult, tiresome
plein (m) – (here) fill it up (with petrol)
pneu (m) – tyre
pneu crevé – puncture
traverser – to cross
vérifier – to check

2
appel (m) de
  détresse – distress call
aussitôt – immediately
averti – warned
capter – to obtain, (here, to pick up)
émetteur (m) – (radio) transmitter
exprimer – to express
inutilisable – unusable
lancer – (here) to put out
ministère (m) ministry
moyens (m pl) – measures
porte-parole (m) – spokesman
préciser – to state
rescapé (m) – survivor
sain et sauf – safe and sound
secours (m) – help
sud (m) – south
tempête (f) – sandstorm
  de sable

GRAMMAR

Verb + à + infinitive

Some verbs are linked to a following infinitive by 'à'.

Here are the commonest:

> apprendre – to learn
> commencer – to begin
> continuer – to continue, to go on
> inviter – to invite
> réussir – to succeed
> se décider – to make up one's mind
> se mettre – to begin

EXAMPLE:
Il a commencé à pleuvoir.
It began to rain.

Les enfants ont continué à jouer.
The children went on playing

- NOTE this construction with 'apprendre':
  J'apprends à nager à mon petit frère.
  I am teaching my little brother to swim.

Other words linked to an infinitive by 'à'

prêt – ready
occupé – busy
EXAMPLE:
Nous sommes prêts à partir.
We are ready to leave.

Il est occupé à faire ses devoirs.
He is busy doing his homework.

- The following useful expressions should also be learned:
  quelque chose à – something to
    manger/boire   eat/drink
  beaucoup à faire – a lot to do
  donner à manger – to feed (animals etc.)

Translating 'by'

1. **'De'** – when following an adjective (or a past participle used as an adjective)
   EXAMPLE:
   La maison était entourée d'arbres.
   The house was surrounded by trees.
   - Note also:
     couvert de   covered by, with
     plein de   full of
     rempli de   full of

2. **'Par'** – in a passive statement
   EXAMPLE:
   J'ai été mordu par un chien.
   I was bitten by a dog.

   - Note the difference between this sort of sentence and the example in no. 1.
     In no. 1 the trees were not actually doing anything, they were merely there.
     In no. 2 the dog was most definitely doing something.

3. **'En'** – with a present participle
   EXAMPLE:
   En prenant le train de six heures tu arriveras avant midi.
   By taking the six o'clock train you will arrive before midday.

4. **'De'**
   EXAMPLE:
   une pièce de Shakespeare
   a play by Shakespeare

   un roman de Dickens
   a novel by Dickens

5. **'Sur'** – in measurements
   EXAMPLE:
   trois mètres de long sur deux mètres de large
   three metres long by two metres wide

6. **Other expressions with 'by'**:
   un à un   one by one
   côte à côte side by side
   par coeur   by heart

7. **'By' in transport expressions** – (see page 92, (Dossier 6, 'En Vacances')

Translating 'before'

1 'Avant' – when 'before' refers to time

a 'Avant' + infinitive
EXAMPLE:
avant de partir   before leaving

● Note that this construction translates English sentences such as:
Before he left he said goodbye.
Avant de partir il a dit au revoir.

b 'Avant' + noun
EXAMPLE:
avant mon départ
before my departure (before I left)

avant son retour
before his return (before he returned)

avant son arrivée
before his arrival (before he arrived)

c 'Avant' + time
EXAMPLE:
avant trois heures   before three o'clock

d 'Avant que'
This must be used in sentences similar to no. 1a, but when the two parts of the sentence do not have the same subject.
EXAMPLE:
Before I left he said goodbye

In French, this type of sentence requires a special part of the verb – the subjunctive, which you do not know, so avoid attempting this sort of sentence in your essay and letter writing.

2 'Devant' – when referring to place
EXAMPLE:
devant la mairie
in front of (or outside) the townhall

'Auparavant' – when 'before' means 'previously'
EXAMPLE:
Il avait visité Paris trois ans auparavant.
He had visited Paris three years previously.

'Déjà' – when 'before' means 'already'
EXAMPLE:
Est-ce que tu as déjà vu ce film?
Have you seen this film before?

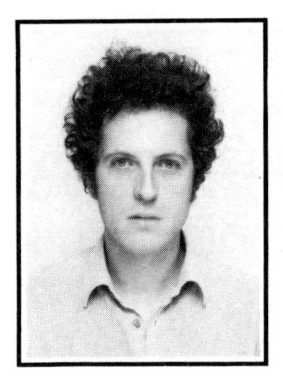

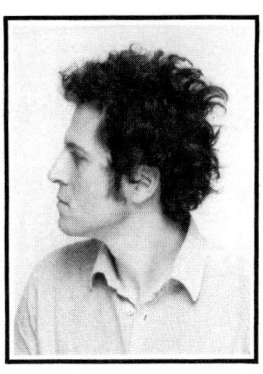

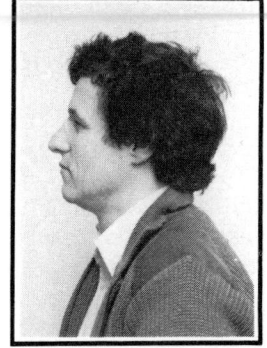

DOSSIER 9

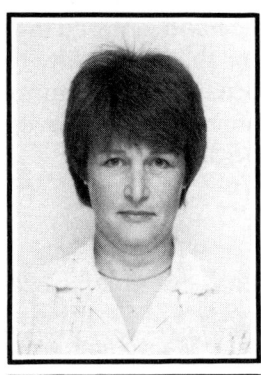

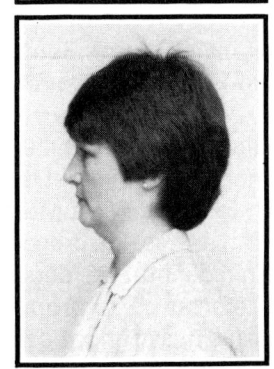

AU VOLEUR!

READING COMPREHENSION

1

On n'est jamais trop jeune . . .

L'histoire a commencé par un petit billet adressé à l'Industrial Bank of Washington : LAISSEZ 10 000 DOLLARS DEVANT LA PORTE PRINCIPALE DE LA BANQUE A HUIT HEURES CE SOIR, SANS QUOI . . .

La police a réussi à appréhender les auteurs de cette tentative d'extorsion, quatre jeunes, âgés de huit à onze ans, au moment où ils venaient récupérer leur butin sur leurs planches à roulettes.

Les racketteurs en culottes courtes ont été remis à leurs parents.

a Where was the money to be left, and when?
b Between what ages were the criminals?
c When were they caught?
d How were they travelling?
e What were they wearing?

2

HOLD-UP ECLAIR A PERPIGNAN

100 000F de butin

Hier mercredi, la chaleur a Perpignan n'a pas découragé les criminels. Un individu s'est présenté dans une Caisse d'Epargne de la ville au moment où celle-ci allait fermer. Habillé d'un survêtement bleu, capuche rabattue, lunettes de soleil, et pistolet à la main, il s'est fait remettre la somme de 100 000F contenue dans les coffres.
Les deux employés ont vu l'homme en question partir à pied et se perdre dans la foule, le sac contenant les 100 000F à la main.

Study the previous newspaper report carefully, then translate the following text into French:

Yesterday, Tuesday, an individual wearing a blue tracksuit with the hood pulled down, and with a pistol in his hand, entered the Banque Populaire and took the sum of fifty thousand francs contained in the safe. An employee of the bank saw the man in question leave on foot and mingle in the crowd.

3

Dans l'obscurité de la chambre Morel attendait près de la fenêtre ouverte. Le sac, plein des objets qu'il avait volés, était sur la petite table à côté de lui. Tout à coup il a entendu une voix qui chuchotait.
Il s'est penché par la fenêtre.
‹C'est toi, Jules?› a-t-il demandé à voix basse.
‹Oui›.
Morel a fait descendre le sac au bout d'une ficelle, puis il a attaché une corde au grand lit en chêne. Doucement, avec précaution, il s'est laissé glisser en bas.
‹Jules, où es-tu?›
Pas de réponse.
‹Jules!›
C'était à ce moment qu'il a entendu le moteur d'une voiture.

‹Ah non, ce n'est pas possible!› s'est-il écrié. Ne voulant pas y croire, il s'est mis à courir dans la direction du bruit. Mais c'était trop tard, la voiture était partie.
Et maintenant, il fallait y croire. Seul dans la nuit sombre et silencieuse Morel s'est rendu compte de la triste vérité. Jules, son copain, qu'il connaissait depuis tant d'années, l'avait trompé. Un chien a commencé à aboyer, et des lumières son apparues aux fenêtres. Mais Morel n'y faisait pas attention. Il s'est assis sur un banc, la tête dans les mains, découragé, déçu. C'était là que deux agents, alertés par le propriétaire, l'ont trouvé. Ils lui ont mis des menottes aux poignets et l'ont emmené. Il n'a offert aucune résistance.

Answer in English the following questions:
a Why was Morel in the house?
b Who was Jules?
c How did Morel leave the house?
d What did he hear?
e What was his reaction to this sound?
f What did Morel realise?
g Why was this realisation so sad for him?
h What **two** things now occurred which meant danger for Morel?
i What was his reaction?
k What did he do when the police found him?

Answer in French the following questions:
a Pourquoi Morel se trouvait-il dans cette maison?
b Pourquoi Morel s'est-il servi d'une ficelle?
c Comment Morel a-t-il quitté la maison?
d Qu'est-ce qu'il a entendu?
e Quelle a été sa réaction en entendant ce bruit?
f De quoi s'est-il rendu compte?
g Pourquoi était-il particulièrement triste en se rendant compte de la vérité?
h Qu'est-ce qui est arrivé qui était dangereux pour Morel? (deux choses)
i Comment les deux agents ont-ils pu trouver Morel?
j Est-ce que Morel s'est battu avec les policiers?

4

L'INVRAISEMBLABLE CAMBRIOLAGE DE ST GELY

Décidément, de nos jours, les cambrioleurs ont de l'imagination. En voici la preuve. Cette histoire, survenue dernièrement à St Gély pourrait passer pour une belle pièce d'humour noir si elle n'était pas aussi odieuse.

Le 21 juillet dernier, Monsieur Maurice Rolland, homme d'affaires d'une cinquantaine d'années, qui demeure dans une villa de St Gély, assiste aux obsèques de sa femme. Quand il rentre chez lui, après la cérémonie, Monsieur Rolland a la mauvaise surprise de trouver sa villa en désordre et vidée de nombreux objets de valeur. Il manque notamment les trois téléviseurs de la maison – dont un en couleur – une chaîne Hi-Fi, des bijoux ayant appartenus à Madame Rolland, des appareils photos et de l'argent. Et, pour couronner le tout, les cambrioleurs sont repartis à bord de la Renault 14 de Monsieur Rolland.

Celui-ci est bouleversé car, visiblement, l'auteur de l'opération savait où était le propriétaire de la villa et de combien de temps il pouvait disposer; on ne déménage pas une telle quantité de matériel sans avoir l'assurance qu'on ne sera pas dérangé.

Monsieur Rolland fit donc appel à un détective privé, en le chargeant de retrouver l'auteur de ce cambriolage particulièrement odieux. Le détective ne fut pas long à identifier le cambrioleur et, surtout, le 'cerveau' de l'opération. Il passe alors ces renseignements à la police, et le lendemain un inspecteur se présente chez... le directeur de l'entreprise de pompes funèbres qui avait réalisé l'enterrement de Madame Rolland!

Celui-ci, Jean-Michel Duffour, trente-cinq ans, avoue rapidement: c'est bien lui qui a organisé le pillage de la villa de Monsieur Rolland, et il ne pouvait être mieux placé pour savoir à quelle heure ce dernier serait absent de son domicile.
De plus, Duffour avait un alibi absolument inattaquable: c'est lui-même qui conduisait le corbillard de Madame Rolland. Et pendant ce temps, un homme bien connu des services de police, Galileo Magnifici, trente ans, cambriolait tranquillement la villa. Magnifici a été arrêté lui aussi et une bonne partie du butin a pu être récupérée dans un garage que Duffour louait au centre de Montpellier.

Il est encore trop tôt pour dire si le directeur de l'entreprise des pompes funèbres avait déjà organisé ce genre d'opération. Mais on ne peut s'empêcher de remarquer qu'il habitait une villa de grand luxe sur la côte méditérranéenne et qu'il possédait plusieurs voitures, dont une 'Jaguar' et un modèle américain.

Answer in English the following questions:
a What was Monsieur Rolland doing on 21st July?
b What exactly had been stolen?
c How had the thief, or thieves, made a getaway?
d Who did Monsieur Rolland ask to solve the mystery?
e Who was the 'brains' behind the crime?
f What was this person's alibi?
g What are you told about the person who actually carried out the robbery?
h What seems to suggest that this was not the first crime masterminded in this way?

Translate into English from 'Monsieur Rolland fit donc appel...' down to '...au centre de Montpellier.'

117

LISTENING COMPREHENSION

1

Listen carefully to the passage before answering in English the following questions:

a Why were Philippe's parents not at home?
b Why was Philippe not with them?
c At what time did he finish his homework?
d How did he spend the rest of the evening?
e What **two** things did he do before going to bed?
f What **two** sounds first made him think that someone was downstairs?
g What sound was then heard?
h What did he do before going downstairs?
i What did he see downstairs that was unexpected?
j Who telephoned the police?
k Which rooms did the police examine?
l Why did Philippe spend the rest of the night at the neighbours' house?

2

Listen carefully to the passage before answering in English the following questions:
a On what day and at what time was Venturini about to close his shop?
b Why had he not sold much that day?
c Where was his wife at closing time?
d Where did she go, on hearing a shout?
e Describe the man she saw there
f What did he appear to be brandishing?
g Where did Mme. Venturini go then?
h Why did she go there?
i What happened to Venturini after the doctor arrived?
j What did the thief make off with?

GRAMMAR EXERCISES

1

Translate these sentences into French:
a She is about twenty years old.
b I noticed a boy with curly hair.
c Monsieur Dubois left the office with his briefcase in his hand.
d The plates fell on the ground.
e The little boy was looking out of the window.
f I remember the day when it began to snow.
g We are looking for some leaflets about Paris.
h He jumped over the wall.

118

2. Write out the passage, choosing the correct word or words from each box.

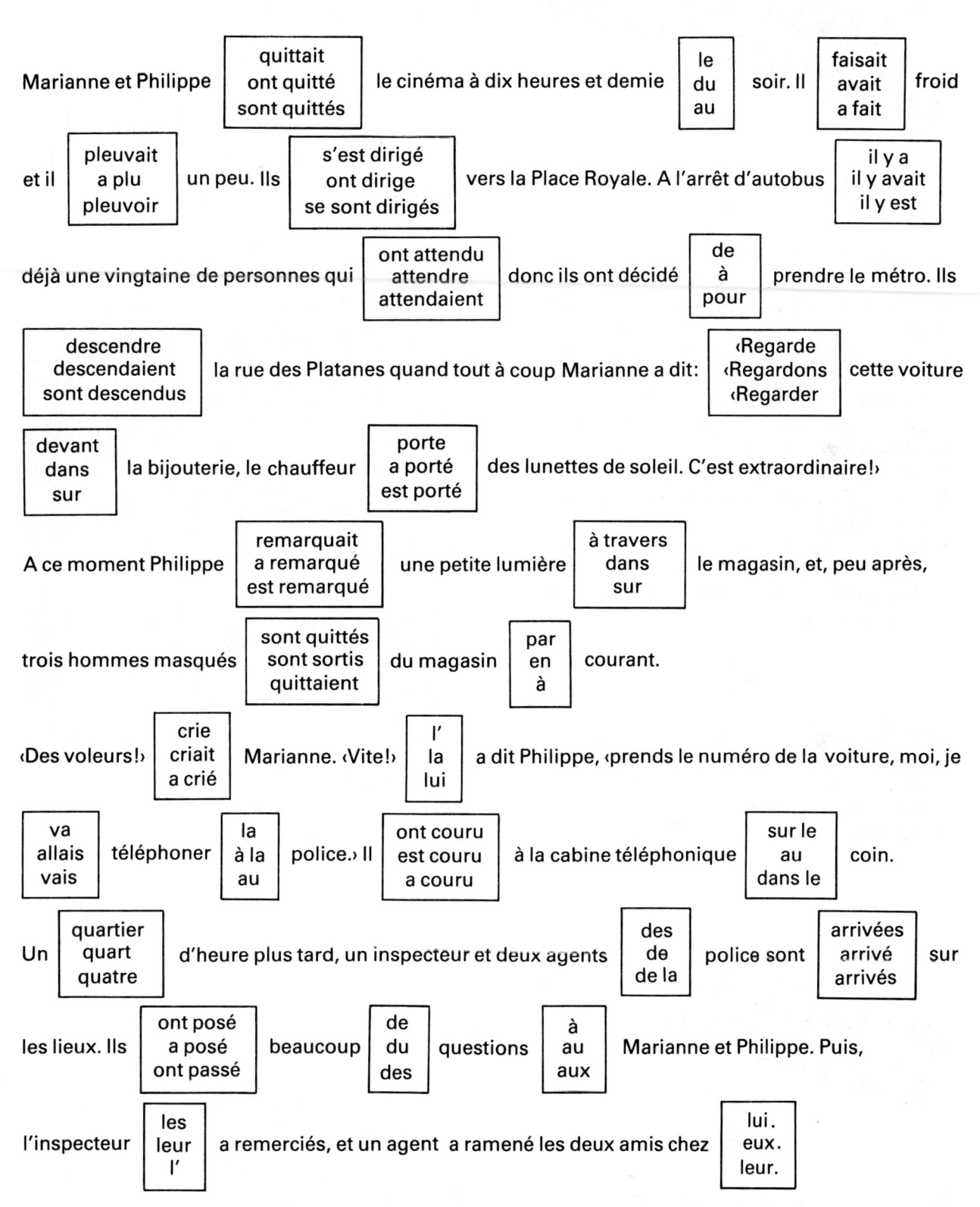

Marianne et Philippe [quittait / ont quitté / sont quittés] le cinéma à dix heures et demie [le / du / au] soir. Il [faisait / avait / a fait] froid et il [pleuvait / a plu / pleuvoir] un peu. Ils [s'est dirigé / ont dirige / se sont dirigés] vers la Place Royale. A l'arrêt d'autobus [il y a / il y avait / il y est] déjà une vingtaine de personnes qui [ont attendu / attendre / attendaient] donc ils ont décidé [de / à / pour] prendre le métro. Ils [descendre / descendaient / sont descendus] la rue des Platanes quand tout à coup Marianne a dit: [«Regarde / «Regardons / «Regarder] cette voiture [devant / dans / sur] la bijouterie, le chauffeur [porte / a porté / est porté] des lunettes de soleil. C'est extraordinaire!»

A ce moment Philippe [remarquait / a remarqué / est remarqué] une petite lumière [à travers / dans / sur] le magasin, et, peu après, trois hommes masqués [sont quittés / sont sortis / quittaient] du magasin [par / en / à] courant.

«Des voleurs!» [crie / criait / a crié] Marianne. «Vite!» [l' / la / lui] a dit Philippe, «prends le numéro de la voiture, moi, je [va / allais / vais] téléphoner [la / à la / au] police.» Il [ont couru / est couru / a couru] à la cabine téléphonique [sur le / au / dans le] coin. Un [quartier / quart / quatre] d'heure plus tard, un inspecteur et deux agents [des / de / de la] police sont [arrivées / arrivé / arrivés] sur les lieux. Ils [ont posé / a posé / ont passé] beaucoup [de / du / des] questions [à / au / aux] Marianne et Philippe. Puis, l'inspecteur [les / leur / l'] a remerciés, et un agent a ramené les deux amis chez [lui. / eux. / leur.]

119

TRAVAIL ORAL

Exercises 1 and 2 should be done **after** completion of exercise 2, 'Marianne et Philippe', in the GRAMMAR EXERCISES section.

1

Vous êtes Marianne (ou Philippe). Répondez aux questions posées par monsieur l'inspecteur.
a A quelle heure avez-vous quitté le cinéma?
b Qu'est-ce que vous avez fait ensuite?
c Pourquoi n'avez-vous pas attendu l'autobus?
d Décrivez la voiture que vous avez vue devant la bijouterie.
e Comment était le chauffeur de la voiture?
f Avez-vous vu autre chose qui vous a frappé?
g Combien d'hommes sont sortis du magasin?
h Qu'est-ce que vous avez fait ensuite?
i Vous avez autre chose à me raconter sur cette affaire?

2

The following day you are interviewed by a reporter from the local newspaper. Relate what happened the previous evening. Make the incident sound as exciting as possible – you want the newspaper to print the story!

3

Attaque !

Look at the cartoon and answer in French the following questions:

a Décrivez le voleur.
b Décrivez le monsieur avec le chien.
c Est-ce que le voleur a peur? Pourquoi pas?
d Racontez la fin de cet incident.

4

Look at the cartoon and answer in French questions a–f.

a Où se passe cette scène?
b Qui parle au téléphone?
c Que fait l'autre voleur?
d Qu'est-ce qu'il y a par terre?
e Où est Monsieur Lenoir?
f Qu'est-ce qu'il porte sur la bouche?
g Translate the caption into English.

Monsieur Lenoir ne peut pas vous répondre . . . Mais si vous voulez mon avis, je n'ai pas l'impression qu'il pourra vous régler ce mois-ci!

TRAVAIL ECRIT

1

Relate the story which the pictures suggest to you.

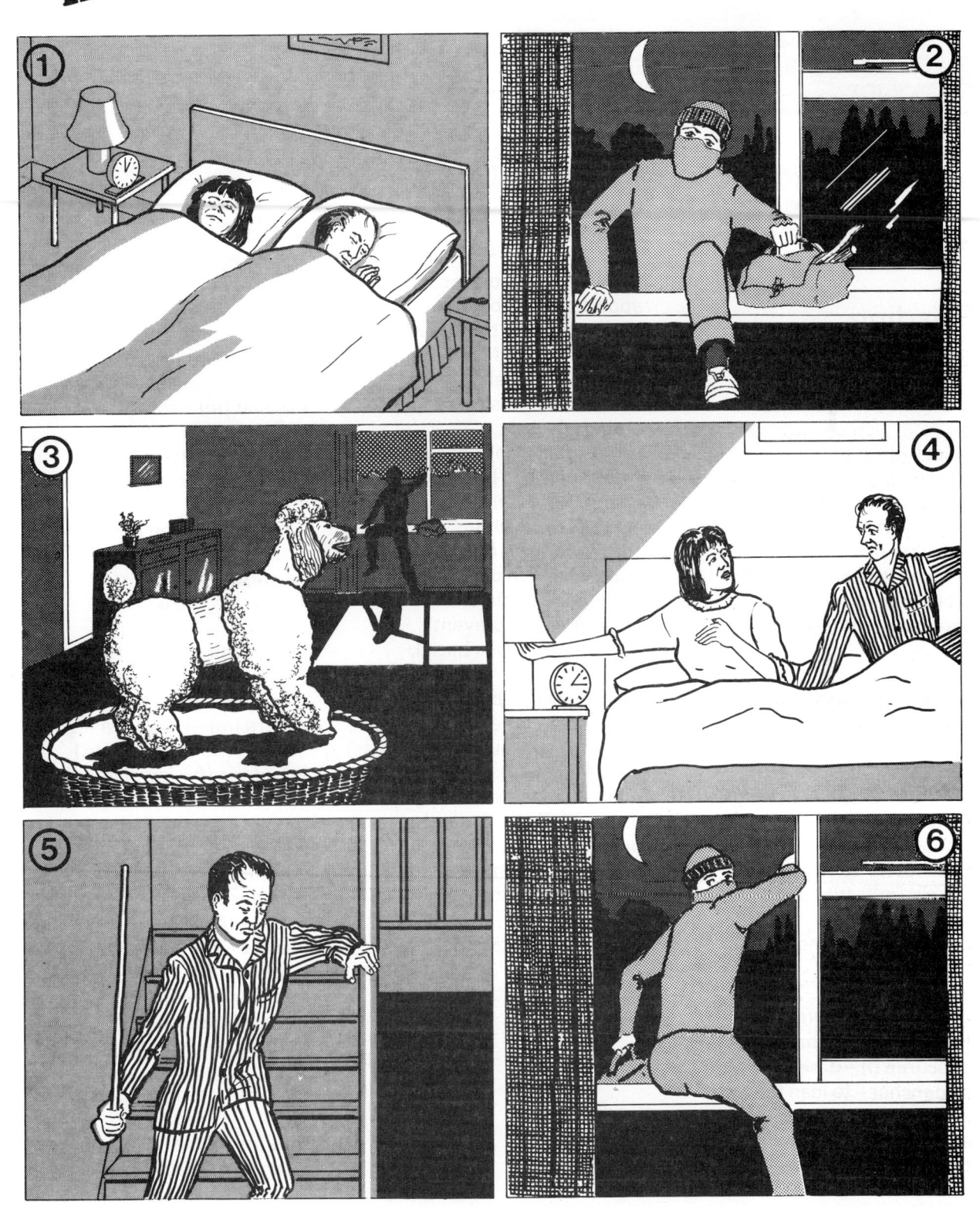

2

Write a story to fit this newspaper headline:

> UN VOL AUDACIEUX: LES MALFAITEURS PRENNENT LA FUITE DANS UNE VOITURE DE POLICE

3

Your neighbour's house was burgled last week. Write a letter to your French penfriend telling him/her what happened.

VOCABULARY

Reading comprehension

1

billet (*m*) – note
culottes (*f pl*) – shorts, short courtes trousers
histoire (*f*) – story
planche (*f*) à roulettes – skateboard
récupérer – to collect
sans quoi – otherwise

2

chaleur (*f*) – heat
foule (*f*) – crowd
survêtement (*m*) – tracksuit

3

banc (*m*) – bench
chêne (*m*) – oak
chuchoter – to whisper
copain (*m*) – friend, pal
corde (*f*) – rope
déçu – disappointed
ficelle (*f*) – string
glisser – to slide
laisser – to let, allow
menottes (*f pl*) – handcuffs
obscurité (*f*) – darkness
se pencher – to lean forward
poignet (*m*) – wrist
se rendre compte – to realise
tromper – to deceive

4

appareil (*m*) photo – camera
appartenir – to belong
assister (à) – to be present (at)
avouer – to confess
bijou (*m*) – jewel
bouleversé – distressed, upset
butin (*m*) – loot
cambriolage (*m*) – burglary
cambrioler – to burgle
cambrioleur (*m*) – burglar
cerveau (*m*) – brain
corbillard (*m*) – hearse
couronner – to crown
déranger – to disturb
empêcher – to prevent
enterrement (*m*) – burial, funeral
entreprise (*f*) – business, firm
genre (*m*) – type, sort
homme (*m*) – business man d'affaires
manquer – to be missing
obsèques (*f pl*) – funeral
odieux (*m*), odieuse (*f*) – hateful
preuve (*f*) – proof
privé – private
renseignements (*m pl*) – information
valeur (*f*) – worth, value
vidé – emptied

Listening comprehension

1

aboyer – to bark
bruit (*m*) – noise
escalier (*m*) – staircase
lait (*m*) – milk
pas (*m*) – footstep
rez-de-chaussée (*m*) – ground floor
sur la pointe – on tiptoe des pieds
en sursaut – with a start

2

apercevoir – to see, to notice
s'apprêter – to prepare, to get ready
arrière (*m*) – back (of a building etc.)
bijouterie (*f*) – jeweller's shop
brandir – to lift (a weapon), to brandish
caisse (*f*) – cash-box, till
comptoir (*m*) – counter
s'emparer – to seize, to grab
épouse (*f*) – wife
étendu – stretched out
large – wide
au milieu de – in the middle of
peu – a little
portefeuille (*m*) – wallet
sol (*m*) – ground
tempe (*f*) – temple (part of the face)
trou (*m*) – hole
visage (*m*) – face

GRAMMAR

Verb + de + infinitive

A number of verbs in French are linked to the infinitive which follows by 'de'.

Here is a list of the commonest ones:

> s'arrêter – to stop
> cesser – to stop, to cease
> décider – to decide
> *défendre – to forbid
> *demander – to ask
> *dire – to tell
> empêcher – to stop, to prevent
> essayer – to try
> faire semblant – to pretend
> *ordonner – to order
> oublier – to forget
> *permettre – to permit, to allow
> prier – to beg, to ask
> regretter – to regret

*REMINDER
These verbs take 'à' before the person.
EXAMPLE:
J'ai demandé à mon ami de téléphoner ce soir.
(See page 102, Dossier 7.)
EXAMPLE:
J'ai oublié d'apporter tes disques.
I forgot to bring your records.

Elle faisait semblant de dormir.
She was pretending to be asleep

Other words linked to the infinitive by 'de'

> content – pleased, glad
> heureux – happy
> obligé – obliged, forced
> le temps – the time

EXAMPLE:
Je suis content de te voir.
I am pleased to see you.

Il n'avait pas le temps de nous parler.
He didn't have time to talk to us.

Translating 'about'

1 **'Vers'** – referring to time
   EXAMPLE:
   vers neuf heures   about nine o'clock

2 **'Environ'** – referring to numbers
   EXAMPLE:
   environ trente-cinq élèves   about thirty-five pupils

3 **'—aine' added to certain 'round' numbers**
   EXAMPLE:
   Il y avait une centaine de manifestants dans la rue.
   There were about a hundred demonstrators in the street

   un homme d'une cinquantaine d'années
   a man of about fifty

   Elle approchait la trentaine.
   She was getting on for thirty.

4 **'Sur'**
   EXAMPLE:
   Avez-vous une brochure sur Boulogne?
   Have you got a leaflet about Boulogne?

5 **'Au sujet de'**
   EXAMPLE:
   Elle s'inquiète au sujet de son fils.
   She is worried about her son.

   Elle s'inquiète à son sujet.
   She is worried about him.

6 **'De'**
   EXAMPLE:
   Il a parlé de son enfance en Normandie.
   He talked about his childhood in Normandy.

More prepositions

1 Translating 'on'
sur la table — on the table
à mon retour — on my return
par un beau jour d'été — on a fine summer's day
par terre — on the ground
le jour où — the day on which (the day when)
lundi — on Monday
le lundi — on Mondays
le 14 juillet — on July 14th

2 Translating 'over'
au-dessus de — over (position)
EXAMPLE:
Le tableau était accroché au-dessus de la cheminée.
The picture was hanging over the fireplace.

par-dessus — over (direction)
EXAMPLE:
Elle a regardé par-dessus le mur.
She looked over the wall.

- Note also:
  par la fenêtre — out of the window

3 Translating 'with'
usually 'avec'.
EXAMPLE:
avec moi — with me

- But note the following expressions:
la jeune fille aux cheveux blonds
the girl with fair hair

l'homme au nez rouge
the man with a red nose

sa valise à la main
with her suitcase in her hand

DOSSIER 10
AU SECOURS!

READING COMPREHENSION

1

a To whom is this article addressed?
b What, according to the article, is often the root cause of accidents?
c What is the first piece of advice given?
d What should you always take with you?
e Which piece of advice is especially important for beginners?
f What is the last piece of advice given?
g What should you always do before leaving?
h What must you do if you change your destination?

Si vous aimez faire de la voile pendant vos vacances, rappelez-vous que les accidents de plaisance constituent 80% de tous les accidents se produisant en mer. L'imprudence est souvent à l'origine. Alors, quelques conseils . . .
Renseignez-vous sur le temps. Un beau temps peut changer brusquement, surtout en mer.
Ne partez jamais en mer sans gilet de sauvetage.
Na naviguez pas trop loin de la côte, surtout si vous êtes débutant dans ce sport.
Un dernier conseil: ne partez jamais seul. Et en tout cas dites toujours que vous partez et où vous allez. Si vous êtes détourné sur un autre port téléphonez pour dire que vous êtes arrivé.

2

Deux taureaux échappant à leurs guardiens au cours d'un défilé pendant les fêtes du quinze août à Arles ont semé la panique dimanche après-midi.
Après avoir traversé au galop un vieux pont sur le Rhône, ils ont pénétré dans le centre-ville, semant sur leur passage la panique parmi la population et les nombreux touristes attablés aux terrasses des cafés.
Au terme d'une poursuite mouvementée qui a duré une heure, les deux taureaux ont été capturés au lasso par les guardiens
De nombreuses voitures en stationnement ont été cabossées.

a What were the bulls taking part in at the time of their escape?
b When did these events occur?
c What route did the bulls take before reaching the town centre?
d Where were the tourists?
e How long did the chase last?
f How were the animals finally caught and by whom?
g What damage was caused?

3

RESCUED FROM THE SNOW

‹Monsieur Papoz! Ouvrez!›
Personne ne répondit. Nous appelâmes tous ensemble.
‹Vite! Ouvrez-nous!›
Un rayon de lumière filtra à travers les volets de bois. Une fenêtre s'ouvrit.
‹Qu'y a-t-il? Le feu?›
Puis, nous reconnaissant dans la lueur de la lanterne, le vieux Papoz s'écria:
‹Ah! c'est vous, les garçons! Que se passe-t-il?›
‹Nous venons de trouver une enfant, une petite fille, dans la neige. Elle a perdu connaissance. Ouvrez!›
La fenêtre se referma. On entendit un bruit de pas précipités, puis des voix. Le père Papoz et sa femme apparurent à la porte.
‹Ciel!› s'écria la fermière en apercevant le corps inerte, ‹une petite fille! Elle est comme morte!›
On nous fit entrer dans la cuisine, une vaste

pièce au plafond bas, où les paysans dressaient leur lit, l'hiver, pour avoir plus chaud.
‹François›, commanda la vieille femme à son mari, ‹ranime le feu pendant que je prépare le lit dans la chambre du fils, puisqu'elle est inoccupée.›
Le père Papoz sortit et revint avec du bois sec, qui commença vite à flamber dans la cendre encore chaude.

Answer in English the following questions:
a What was the first thought Monsieur Papoz had of what might be wrong?
b Where had the boys found the child?
c What state was she in?
d What **two** noises were heard after the window closed?
e Into which room were the boys taken?
f What are you told about this room?
g Why did the farmer and his wife put their bed in there?
h What did the old woman tell her husband to do?
i Which room was she going to prepare for the child, and why?
j Why did the wood on the fire start burning quickly?

Translate from 'La fenêtre se referma ...' to the end of the passage.

Answer in French the following questions, but **do not** use the past historic tense in your answers:
a Qu'est-ce que les garçons ont demandé à Monsieur Papoz de faire?
b Qu'est-ce que les garçons venaient de trouver?
c Comment était la cuisine?
d Pourquoi les paysans dressaient-ils leur lit dans la cuisine?
e Qu'est-ce que la vieille femme allait faire?
f Qu'est-ce que le père Papoz est allé chercher?

4

The following passage is the opening pages of *L'Astragale*, a novel by Albertine Sarrazin. The author (who tragically died at the age of thirty) never knew her real parents, and was brought up by foster parents. She was an extremely intelligent girl, but difficult and rebellious. She spent much of her time in the French equivalent

127

of Borstal, and at the age of eighteen was sent to prison. She escaped, by climbing over a wall. *L'Astragale*, published in 1965, is the story, in fictional form, of her own experiences.

◀ Je m'étais dit que le mur n'était pas très haut. (Quelle folie!) Je lâchai prise. Je tombai. Je restais assise pour laisser passer le choc. Ma main quitta le sol, passa sur mon bras gauche, remonta jusqu'à l'épaule, descendit jusqu'aux hanches. J'étais intacte, je pouvais continuer. Je me mis debout – et mon nez heurta douloureusement contre la terre. J'avais oublié de vérifier aussi mes jambes. Eh bien, puisque les jambes sont inutiles, je vais marcher sur les coudes et les genoux. Je rampe. Les coudes et les genoux saignent. J'ai mal, mais il faut continuer à avancer, au moins jusqu'à cette lumière, là-bas, qui me promet la route. Enfin, la voilà, la route. Je vais commencer à faire de l'autostop ici. Non, Paris est dans la direction opposée, il faut traverser. Je fais cinq mètres, je n'en peux plus. La première voiture qui viendra, elle va m'écraser. Mais je n'y peux rien. J'attends. Et voilà une voiture qui arrive. Je regarde ses gros phares jaunes. J'entends grincer les freins. La voiture stoppe, la portière claque, des pas s'approchent.
‹Mademoiselle?›
Je dis: ‹Si vous voulez, sortez-moi de la route. Tenez-moi, je crois que j'ai une jambe cassée!› Doucement, il me prend les bras. Je réussis à me traîner jusqu'au bord de la route.
‹Qu'est-ce qui vous est arrivé?›
‹Je . . . (mais pourquoi mentir, ce n'est pas la peine).›
‹Vous connaissez le coin?›
‹Oui.›
‹Alors vous savez peut-être ce qu'il y a là-bas?›
‹Euh . . . Oui. Et c'est de là . . . ?›
‹Oui, à l'instant, enfin, il y a une demi-heure. On ne doit pas me chercher encore. Oh, je vous prie, emmenez-moi à Paris. Vous n'aurez pas d'ennuis, je vous promets. A Paris vous me déposez, et je me débrouille.›
‹Montre un peu ce pied,› dit-il.
L'homme s'accroupit devant moi, il promèna la lumière d'une lampe de poche. Puis il se redressa, et éteignit la lampe. Un bras entoura mes épaules, un autre se glissa sous mes genoux, je fus soulevée, emportée. L'inconnu s'engagea dans un petit chemin, fit une centaine de mètres, et me déposa par terre avec précaution.

‹Attends là,› dit-il, ‹et surtout ne bouge pas. Je vais revenir te chercher, attends-moi.›
Et il s'éloigna.
Le temps passe. Une heure, deux. Je ne sais pas. Je grelotte de froid. L'herbe est trempée. Je rampe quelques mètres. Je m'affale de nouveau. Quelqu'un s'approche. C'est lui.
‹Je t'avais pourtant dit de ne pas bouger!›
‹J'ai bougé? C'est possible. Je ne me rappelle pas.›
‹Tiens, dit-il, j'ai apporté un pantalon et un pull. Il y a aussi du sparadrap.›
‹Merci. Comment t'appelles-tu?›
‹Julien. Et toi?›
‹Anne.›
‹Voilà, Anne, des chaussettes en laine. Essaie de les mettre.›
‹Oh non! par pitié! Ça fait trop mal. Je resterai pieds nus.›
‹Comme tu veux. Je vais te porter sur la moto. Tu sais aller à moto?›
‹Oui, j'ai l'habitude. Maintenant, partons!›
Il me lève, me dépose doucement sur la moto. Je laisse mon pied pendre à côté de la roue, et je m'ancre à deux bras aux épaules de Julien. Une autre vie commence. ▶

Answer in English the following questions:
a   Where precisely is Anne in the first sentence of the passage?
b   What does she do as she sits on the ground, and why?
c   How does she decide to move?
d   What does she want to reach?
e   Why must she cross the road?
    What does she first ask the motorist to do?
g   According to Anne, how long is it since she made her escape?
h   What **two** things does the motorist tell Anne to do before he leaves?
i   What does Anne tell us about her condition at this point?
j   State **three** things Julien has brought her.
k   Why does she refuse to put on the woollen socks?
l   How are they going to travel?
m   'L'astragale' is the medical name for a certain bone in the ankle. Can you now suggest why it is the title of this book?

Translate into English from 'Le temps passe . . .' to the end of the passage.

128

LISTENING COMPREHENSION

1

Listen carefully to the passage before answering in English the following questions:
a On what day and at what time did this incident occur?
b What was the car driver trying to do?
c Why was this particularly difficult?
d What did he damage?
e Who gave the alarm?
f Name the **three** groups of people who answered the alarm call.
g For how long were people evacuated from their homes?
h What are we told about injuries?

2

Listen carefully to the passage before answering in English the following questions:
a What age is the child?
b From where did she fall?
c Where was Tatiana before her fall, and what was she doing?
d Where was her mother?
e What did the child do which caused her to fall?
f Explain exactly how she landed.
g Why is she being kept in hospital?

3

Listen carefully to the passage before answering in English the following questions:
a When exactly did this accident occur?
b What sort of zoo is the one at Sigean?
c In what part of the zoo were Mr and Mrs Stevens when the accident occurred?
d In what way were they breaking the regulations?
e What were the cars doing when the accident occurred?
f How, precisely, did the accident happen?
g What injury did Mrs Stevens receive?
h Where was she taken?

4

A boy is kidnapped in Sardinia

Listen carefully to the passage before answering in English the following questions:
a When was Silvio Maso kidnapped?
b Who was in the car with him?
c What colour was the kidnappers' car?
d How many kidnappers were there?

e Who is Mario Santuzzi?
f How old is he?
g How many sheep does he have?
h Describe the shepherd's hut.
i What was the weather like that Saturday evening? (**two** things)
j What was Santuzzi doing when he heard someone at the door?
k What **two** things does he say about the boy's condition?
l How had Silvio escaped?
m At what time of day?
n Name **two** things the guards were doing at the time?
o What noise was heard?
p Where exactly did Santuzzi hide Silvio?

q How many men were at the door?
r What did they ask?
s Where did Santuzzi take them?
t Why did he ask them not to frighten the animals?

u What did Santuzzi tell Silvio to do?
v How far was the village from Santuzzi's hut?
w How many policemen returned to the hut with him?
x What did Silvio's family invite Santuzzi and the policemen to do?
y What was Santuzzi given?
z What was his comment?

129

GRAMMAR EXERCISES

1

Translate these sentences into French:
a She took a knife to cut the meat.
b He left without saying anything.
c Without hesitating the thief jumped through the window.
d You should help your mother instead of watching television.
e I am too tired to go out this evening.
f My uncle has just arrived from New York.
g After finishing his breakfast, he decided to go for a walk.
h Without wasting any time we telephoned the doctor.
i It is too late to go to the cinema now.
j Instead of walking they took a taxi.

TRAVAIL ORAL

1

Continue the story of **one** of the openings given below. Think out carefully what you are going to say, but don't write anything down.
Remember to use past tenses.

a Je faisais mes devoirs hier soir quand tout à coup ma mère a poussé un cri. Je me suis précipité dans la cuisine et j'ai vu que la poêle avait pris feu . . .

b Je rentrais du collège hier après-midi avec mon copain Marc. Il y avait une vieille dame qui marchait juste devant nous. Soudain, elle a glissé, (le trottoir était un peu mouillé) et elle est tombée par terre . . .

c Je suis rentré du collège hier à quatre heures et demie. Devant la porte j'ai cherché ma clef dans ma poche. Elle n'y était pas. Je l'avais oubliée, ou je l'avais perdue! Je savais que mes parents allaient passer la soirée en ville et les voisins étaient en vacances. Que faire?

2

Relate a story which the following pictures suggest to you.

TRAVAIL ECRIT

1 Write a story which **one** of the following newspaper headlines suggests to you:
(120 words)

a
ACCIDENT DE MONTAGNE
Un jeune skieur sauvé par un chien

c
UN GARCON DE NEUF ANS TOMBE D'UN ARBRE
Il essayait de sauver un chaton.

b
UN INCENDIE A DOMICILE
Une Poêle Prend Feu

2 Last week a fire occurred in either **a** the house next door, or **b** the flat above yours. Write a letter to your French penfriend, telling him/her what happened.
(150 words)

3 Write the story suggested by the pictures in the TRAVAIL ORAL section.

VOCABULARY

Reading comprehension

1
brusquement – suddenly
conseil (m) – advice
côte (f) – coast, shore
débutant (m) – beginner
faire de la voile – to go sailing
gilet (m) de sauvetage – life-jacket
imprudence (f) – foolishness, carelessness
plaisance (f) – yachting, sailing
se renseigner – to find out, to inform oneself

2
attablé – sitting at a table
cabosser – to dent, bash in
défilé (m) – procession
pont (m) – bridge
poursuite (f) – chase
semer – to sow, (here) to cause
taureau (m) – bull
au terme de – at the end of
traverser – to cross

3
bas – low
cendre (f) – ash
fermière (f) – farmer's wife
feu (m) – fire
flamber – to flame, burn
inoccupé – unoccupied, vacant
lueur (f) – gleam, faint light
pas (m) – step
se passer – to happen
perdre connaisance – to faint
plafond (m) – ceiling
précipité – hurried
rayon (m) – ray
sec – dry
à travers – through, across
volet (m) – shutter

4
s'accroupir – to crouch down
s'affaler – to fall, to collapse
bouger – to move
ce n'est pas la peine – it's not worth it
claquer – to slam
coin (m) – (here) district, area
coude (m) – elbow

131

courir – to run
se débrouiller – to cope, to manage
écraser – to run over
s'éloigner – to go away, to move away
éteindre – to put out (a light)
faire de l'autostop – to hitch-hike
grelotter – to shiver
grincer – to creak, to grind
heurter – to bump, to crash
lâcher prise – to let go
mentir – to lie
montrer – to show
mur (*m*) – wall
pendre – to hang
phare (*m*) – headlight
pieds nus – barefoot
ramper – to crawl
se redresser – to stand up
réussir – to succeed
roue (*f*) – wheel
sol (*m*) – ground, earth
soulever – to lift up
sparadrap (*m*) – sticking-plaster, Elastoplast
terre (*f*) – earth
se traîner – to drag oneself
trempé – soaked
vérifier – to check

Listening comprehension

1

affolé – panic-stricken
faire demi-tour – to make a U-turn
ne . . . aucun – no, not any
signaler – to announce
sur les lieux – at the scene (of an accident, crime)

2

atterrir – to land
blessure (*f*) – wound
buisson (*m*) – bush
étendre – to spread
fil (*m*) – cord, thread
garder – to keep
linge (*m*) – washing
moindre – least, smallest
se pencher – to lean (forward)

3

abaisser – to lower
attirer – to attract
début (*m*) – beginning
mordre – to bite
ours (*m*) – bear
parmi – among
portière (*f*) – door (of car, train)
règlement (*m*) – regulation
vitre (*f*) – pane (of glass)

4

agneau (*m*) – lamb
aîné – elder, eldest
appuyé – leaning
bâtiment (*m*) – building
berger (*m*) – shepherd
bergerie (*f*) – shepherd's hut
bête (*f*) – animal
brebis (*f*) – ewe, female sheep
cacher – to hide
camionnette (*f*) – van
s'échapper – to escape
effrayer – to frighten
enclos (*m*) – enclosure
mettre bas – to give birth (animals)
moteur (*m*) – engine
mouton (*m*) – sheep
mort – dead
paille (*f*) – straw
pétrole (*f*) – paraffin
pousser – to push
prendre un verre – to have a drink
station (*f*) – holiday resort
suite (*f*) – sequel, what follows
tirer – to pull, drag
à toute vitesse – at top speed
type (*m*) – fellow, man

GRAMMAR

The past historic tense

This is a past tense which is used only in written, literary French, such as novels, short stories, biographies, etc. At this stage, you only need to be able to recognise it for purposes of translation and comprehension. You do not need to write it yourself.

Here are the forms of the past historic:

1 All —er verbs take the following endings:

—ai	—âmes
—as	—âtes
—a	—èrent

EXAMPLE:
donner – to give
je donnai   I gave
tu donnas
il/elle/on donna
nous donnâmes
vous donnâtes
ils/elles donnèrent

2 The —is endings:

—is	—îmes
—is	—îtes
—it	—irent

EXAMPLE:
attendre – to wait
j'attendis   I waited
tu attendis
il/elle/on attendit
nous attendîmes
vous attendîtes
ils/elles attendirent

Here is a list of common verbs which take the —is endings:

s'asseoir – to sit down   je m'assis
dire – to say, to tell   je dis
dormir – to sleep   je dormis
écrire – to write   j'écrivis
faire – to do, to make   je fis
finir – to finish   je finis
mettre – to put   je mis
ouvrir – to open   j'ouvris
partir – to leave   je partis
prendre – to take   je pris
répondre – to answer   je répondis
rire – to laugh   je ris
sortir – to go out   je sortis
suivre – to follow   je suivis
vendre – to sell   je vendis
voir – to see   je vis

3 The —us endings:

—us	—ûmes
—us	—ûtes
—ut	—urent

EXAMPLE:
courir – to run
je courus   I ran
tu courus
il/elle/on courut
nous courûmes
vous courûtes
ils/elles coururent

Here is a list of common verbs which take the —us endings:

apercevoir – to catch a glimpse of   j'aperçus
avoir – to have   j'eus
boire – to drink   je bus
connaître – to know   je connus
courir – to run   je courus
croire – to believe, to think   je crus
devoir – to have to, must   je dus
être – to be   je fus
lire – to read   je lus
mourir – to die   je mourus
paraître – to seem   je parus
pleuvoir – to rain   il plut
pouvoir – to be able, can   je pus
recevoir – to receive   je reçus
savoir – to know   je sus
vouloir – to want   je voulus

4 Two verbs, 'venir' and 'tenir' (and their compounds), have a special form for their past historic:
je vins
tu vins
il/elle/on vint
nous vînmes
vous vîntes
ils/elles vinrent

Changing direct to indirect speech

This has already been mentioned in the grammar sections of Dossiers 2, 5 and 6, where the changes of tense required were pointed out. It was also pointed out that a change of subject pronoun was usually needed.
EXAMPLE:
Il a dit, 'J'ai perdu la clef.'
becomes:
Il a dit qu'il avait perdu la clef.

Elle a dit, 'J'irai à Paris pendant les vacances.'
becomes:
Elle a dit qu'elle irait à Paris pendant les vacances.

133

These changes may be written out in a table, as follows:

DIRECT SPEECH **becomes** INDIRECT SPEECH

je	il **or** elle
nous	ils **or** elles
tu	je
vous	je **or** nous
il, elle } ils, elles }	stay the same
present tense	imperfect tense
future tense	conditional tense
perfect tense	pluperfect tense

Occasionally, there are exceptions to the above rules for pronoun changes. However, they are rare and are unlikely to concern you at this stage.

Other changes may be necessary.
EXAMPLE:
Il a dit, 'J'ai oublié mon portefeuille.'
becomes:
Il a dit qu'il avait oublié **son** portefeuille.

Ils ont dit, 'Nous avons apporté nos disques.'
becomes:
Ils ont dit qu'ils avaient apporté **leurs** disques.

Elle a dit, 'Je partirai demain.'
becomes:
Elle a dit qu'elle partirait **le lendemain**.

More uses of the infinitive

The following summary contains examples of sentences and phrases which are useful in essay writing. Learn them, and try to introduce them into your written work where appropriate.

1 After 'pour'
EXAMPLE:
Il a pris son stylo pour signer la lettre.
He took his pen (in order) to sign the letter.

Je suis trop fatigué pour travailler ce soir.
I am too tired to work this evening

Je n'ai pas assez d'argent pour acheter ce disque.
I haven't enough money to buy this record.

2 After 'sans'
EXAMPLE:
sans rien dire . . .   without saying anything . . .
sans tarder . . .   without delay . . .
sans perdre de temps . . .   without wasting time . . .
sans hésiter . . .   without hesitating . . .

3 After 'au lieu de . . .'
EXAMPLE:
Tu devrais étudier au lieu de lire des magazines.
You ought to study instead of reading magazines.

Au lieu de me répondre, il a pris le journal.
Instead of answering me, he picked up the newspaper.

4 After 'en train de . . .'
EXAMPLE:
J'étais en train de faire mes devoirs quand il est arrivé.

I was in the middle of (in the act of, busy,) doing my homework when he arrived.

5 After 'venir (present or imperfect tenses) de . . .'
EXAMPLE:
Je viens d'arriver.   I have just arrived.
Il venait de partir.   He had just left.

6 After 'il faut . . .'
EXAMPLE:
Il faut travailler pour réussir.
It is necessary to (you must) work in order to succeed.

REVISION TEST TWO

Grammar

1

Write these sentences putting the verb in brackets into the future tense:

a Demain elle (venir) nous voir.
b Il (aller) au collège l'année prochaine.
c Je (téléphoner) à Philippe ce soir.
d Nous ne (pouvoir) pas vous voir cette semaine.
e Tu (voir) tes cousins demain.
f Ils (sortir) ce soir.
g Vous (avoir) une belle surprise.
h Mon père (être) content.
i A huit heures je (faire) mes devoirs.
j Je ne (savoir) pas quoi faire.

2

Write out the sentences below, filling in the gaps. Each gap will need either:
à; de; par; nothing.

a Je veux — acheter un nouveau stylo.
b Nous avons décidé — faire des courses cet après-midi.
c Pierre était malade, donc il a dû — rester au lit.
d L'année dernière j'ai appris — nager.
e Je lui ai demandé — m'aider.
f Il a commencé — pleuvoir.
g Elle a essayé — ouvrir le paquet.
h Le chien s'est mis — aboyer.
i Ils ont continué — parler.
j Elle a cessé — tricoter.
k Nous avons oublié — fermer les fenêtres.
l Je suis prêt — partir.
m Gisèle était occupée — faire un gâteau.
n Il a enfin réussi — réparer son vélo.
o Les élèves n'osaient pas — parler.
p Tais-toi! Tu m'empêches — travailler.
q Elle est venue — écouter mon nouveau disque.
r Elle a fini — pleurer.
s Je te défends — sortir.
t Il faisait semblant — lire le journal.

3

Translate into French the following sentences, paying particular attention to the use of prepositions:

a I have been waiting for half an hour.
b They arrived about five o'clock.
c I am reading a book by Simenon.
d We shall leave at six o'clock in the morning.
e In the spring, I am going to spend a week in Scotland.
f The mountains were covered with snow.
g They will go to Paris for three days and then they will go to Italy.
h I don't like sitting in the sun, I prefer to stay in the shade.
i In winter I go to school by bus, but in summer I go by bike.
j In my opinion you are wrong.
k When it is raining my father goes to the office by taxi.
l There were about a hundred pupils in the hall.
m Before going out, you must do your homework.
n She looked out of the window.
o I am very pleased to see you.
p She slipped and fell on the ground.
q He lived in France for two years, but now he lives in the United States.
r Have you visited the Eiffel Tower before?
s I bought a pullover for my brother.
t My Aunt Sophie lives in the country.

Vocabulary

1

In the following groups, you must match up each French word with its correct meaning:

le maillot de bain	free of charge
louer	the rate
la baignade	to drink/eat slowly (so as to savour the flavour)
le syndicat d'initiative	to agree
gratuit	bathing
le tarif	swimming costume
déguster	the first aid post
être d'accord	the show
le poste de secours	to hire, rent
le spectacle	the tourist information office

135

2

brumeux	clear period
l'averse	cloudy
l'éclaircie	overcast
nuageux	elsewhere
le brouillard	the traffic jam
couvert	the traffic
l'embouteillage	misty
la circulation	to avoid
éviter	the fog
ailleurs	the shower

3

la grève	the broadcast
le salaire	the driving licence
l'émission	the job
le permis de conduire	the strike
l'emploi	famous
célèbre	the salesman
le pourboire	the tip
le vendeur	the fine
l'infirmière	the wages
l'amende	the tip

4

conduire	the tyre
vérifier	to clean
le parebrise	to check
le pneu	to overtake
nettoyer	to drive
l'affiche	the poster
dépasser	the gear
la pièce de rechange	the spare part
la vitesse	to cross
traverser	the windscreen

5

aboyer	the till
le portefeuille	the burglar
la caisse	the handcuffs
voler	to bark
le cambrioleur	the wallet
vider	to steal
le butin	to disturb
les menottes	to whisper
déranger	the loot
chuchoter	to empty

6

garder	the engine
la portière	the van
affolé	the advice
tirer	to keep
le moteur	to run over
la camionnette	the car door
le conseil	to lie
écraser	panic-stricken
mentir	the headlight
le phare	to pull, drag

Could you cope?

● NOTE
This part of the test revises items from the entire book, not just Dossiers 6–10

Below you will find a selection of things which you might need to say if you were staying in France. How would you get on?

1

Shopping
Ask for:
2 slices of ham
100 grammes of butter
a long French loaf
a bottle of lemonade
a kilo of apples
3 stamps at 1F60
some elastoplast
some aspirins

2

In a café
Order the following:
2 cheese sandwiches
1 ham sandwich
1 cup of coffee
1 beer
1 Coca-Cola

3
At a hotel
Ask if they have two single rooms with shower.
Ask how much the rooms cost.
Ask what time they serve dinner.

4
At the garage
Ask for the car to be filled with 4-star petrol.
Ask for the tyres to be checked.
Ask for the windscreen to be cleaned.

5
In a restaurant
Order the following:
3 roast chicken, 2 with chips and one with salad.
Ask for a bottle of white wine and a bottle of mineral water.

6
At the campsite
Ask what time the swimming pool opens.
Ask if you can hire bicycles.
Ask if the cinema is open this evening.

DOSSIER 11

REFERENCE SECTION

Numbers

1 un, une
2 deux
3 trois
4 quatre
5 cinq
6 six
7 sept
8 huit
9 neuf
10 dix
11 onze
12 douze
13 treize
14 quatorze
15 quinze
16 seize
17 dix-sept
18 dix-huit
19 dix-neuf
20 vingt
21 vingt et un
22 vingt-deux
23 vingt-trois
30 trente
31 trente et un
32 trente-deux
40 quarante
50 cinquante
60 soixante
70 soixante-dix
71 soixante et onze
72 soixante-douze
80 quatre-vingts
81 quatre-vingt-un
90 quatre-vingt-dix
91 quatre-vingt-onze
100 cent
200 deux cents
210 deux cent dix
1000 mille
2000 deux mille

1st   premier, première
2nd deuxième
       second, seconde
       (less commonly used)
3rd   troisième
4th   quatrième

Days, months, seasons

dimanche – Sunday
lundi – Monday
mardi – Tuesday
mercredi – Wednesday
jeudi – Thursday
vendredi – Friday
samedi – Saturday

janvier – January
février – February
mars – March
avril – April
mai – May
juin – June
juillet – July
août – August
septembre – September
octobre – October
novembre – November
décembre – December

le printemps – the Spring
l'été (*m*) – the Summer
l'automne (*m*) – the Autumn
l'hiver (*m*) – the Winter

Dates

le premier mai – May 1st
le deux mai – May 2nd
le quinze août – August 15th
le trente et un juillet – July 31st
lundi, deux mai – Monday, May 2nd
jeudi, quatorze juillet – Thursday, July 14th

Noël – Christmas
Pâques – Easter
la Pentecôte – Whitsun
le jour de l'an – New Year's Day
la veille de Noël – Christmas Eve
la veille du jour de l'an – New Year's Eve

Time

une heure – one o'clock
deux heures – two o'clock
deux heures cinq – five past two
deux heures dix – ten past two
deux heures et quart – quarter past two
deux heures vingt – twenty past two
deux heures vingt-cinq – twenty five past two
deux heures et demie – half past two
trois heures moins vingt-cinq – twenty five to three
trois heures moins vingt – twenty to three
trois heures moins le quart – quarter to three
trois heures moins dix – ten to three
trois heures moins cinq – five to three
midi – twelve o'clock midday
minuit – twelve o'clock midnight

- NOTE:
  midi et demi – half past twelve (midday)
  minuit et demi – half past twelve (midnight)
  } no 'e' on 'demi'

Always use 'il est' 'il était' (**not** c'est, c'était) for telling the time.

The twenty-four hour clock is widely used in France for timetables, announcements, etc.
EXAMPLE:
Le train part à dix-neuf heures.
The train leaves at 19.00 hours.

Time expressions

aujourd'hui – today
demain – tomorrow
après-demain – the day after tomorrow
hier – yesterday
avant-hier – the day before yesterday
le lendemain – the next day
le lendemain matin – the next (following) morning
la veille – the evening (day) before

la semaine – the week
le mois – the month
le siècle – the century
la semaine dernière (passée) – last week
la semaine prochaine – next week
l'an dernier (passé) – last year
l'année dernière (passée) – last year

après une demi-heure – after half an hour (no 'e' on 'demi')
dix minutes plus tard – ten minutes later
au bout d'une demi-heure – after half an hour
une fois, deux fois, etc. – once, twice, etc.
trois fois par jour – three times a day
la prochaine fois – next time
la dernière fois – last time
tous les jours – every day
chaque jour – each day
en même temps – at the same time
le matin – the morning (in the morning)
l'après-midi – the afternoon (in the afternoon)
le soir – the evening (in the evening)
la nuit – the night (at night)
le jour – the day
la journée – the day (duration)
toute la journée – all day long
la matinée – the morning (duration)
la soirée – the evening (duration)
tout à l'heure – presently, just now
bientôt – soon
de bonne heure – early
tôt – early
tôt ou tard – sooner or later
en retard – late (for a definite time)
tard – late

Linking words and expressions

cependant – however
ensuite – then
puis – then
alors – then, consequently
donc – so (=therefore)
car – for (=because)
parce que – because (**but** à cause de – because of)
ainsi – so, thus
pourtant – yet, however
quand, lorsque – when
enfin – at last, finally
d'abord – at first, first of all
pendant que – while (**but** pendant – during)

141

Other useful words and expressions

assez – enough
J'ai assez mangé. – I've had enough to eat.

assez – fairly
Elle est assez grande. – She is fairly tall.

trop – too much
J'ai trop mangé. – I've eaten too much.

trop de – too many
Elle mange trop de bonbons. – She eats too many sweets.

plus de – more than
moins de – less than
soudain – suddenly
tout à coup – suddenly
vite – quickly
lentement – slowly
tout de suite – immediately, at once
immédiatement – immediately
souvent – often
de temps en temps – from time to time
il y a trois jours – three days ago
il y a un mois – a month ago
quelquefois – sometimes
quelque chose (**two** words) – something

Expressions with 'avoir'

avoir chaud – to be hot
avoir froid – to be cold
avoir faim – to be hungry
avoir soif – to be thirsty
avoir peur – to be afraid
avoir raison – to be right
avoir tort – to be wrong
avoir besoin (de) – to need
avoir peur (de) – to be afraid (of)
avoir mal à la tête – to have a headache
J'en ai assez. – I've had enough of it. (I'm fed up with it.)
Qu'y a-t-il? – What's the matter?
Qu'est-ce que tu as? – What's the matter with you?

Expressions with 'faire'

faire la vaisselle – to do the washing up
faire le ménage – to do the housework
faire la lessive – to do the washing
faire des courses – to go shopping
faire une promenade – to go for a walk
faire une promenade à vélo – to go for a bike ride
faire des économies – to save (money)
faire un pique-nique – to go for a picnic
faire de l'auto-stop – to go hitch-hiking
faire une valise – to pack a suitcase
faire le plein – to fill up (with petrol)
Ça ne fait rien – It doesn't matter.
Qu'est-ce qu'il fait dans la vie? – What is his job?
Ne vous en faites pas. – Don't worry.
Il n'y a rien à faire. – There's nothing to be done, it's hopeless.
Ça fait combien? – How much is that?
Que faire? – What can (could) I (he, she anyone) do?

Weather expressions

These are all given in present and imperfect tenses. You should learn both. You will need the present tense for oral work, whereas the imperfect tense will be needed for essays.
Il fait beau. – It is fine.
Il faisait beau. – It was fine.
Il fait mauvais. – It is bad weather.
Il faisait mauvais. – It was bad weather.
Il fait chaud. – It is hot.
Il faisait chaud. – It was hot.
Il fait froid. – It is cold.
Il faisait froid. – It was cold.
Il fait du vent. – It is windy.
Il faisait du vent. – It was windy.
Le soleil brille. – The sun is shining.
Le soleil brillait. – The sun was shining.
Il pleut. – It is raining.
Il pleuvait. – It was raining.
Il neige. – It is snowing.
Il neigeait. – It was snowing.
Il gèle. – It is freezing.
Il gêlait. – It was freezing.
Il fait du brouillard. – It is foggy.
Il faisait du brouillard. – It was foggy.

Adjectives

Adjectives in French must agree with the noun they describe.

1. The regular pattern is as follows:

masculine singular	feminine singular	masculine plural	feminine plural
grand	grande	grands	grandes
petit	petite	petits	petites

2. If the masculine singular ends in 's' or 'z' it is unchanged in the masculine plural.
EXAMPLE:
français   française   français   françaises

3. If the adjective ends in silent 'e' in the masculine singular, it is unchanged in the feminine singular.
EXAMPLE:
rouge   rouge   rouges   rouges

4. Some adjectives double the final consonant before adding 'e'.
bon   bonne   bons   bonnes
gentil   gentille   gentils   gentilles
gros   grosse   gros   grosses

5. Adjectives which end in —er follow this pattern:
cher   chère   chers   chères
premier   première   premiers   premières
dernier   dernière   derniers   dernières

6. Adjectives which end in —x follow this pattern:
délicieux   délicieuse   délicieux   délicieuses
paresseux   paresseuse   paresseux   paresseuses

7. Some adjectives are irregular, and must be learnt by heart. Here are some of the commonest:
long   longue   longs   longues
blanc   blanche   blancs   blanches
sec   sèche   secs   sèches

8. Some adjectives have **two** forms of the masculine singular. The first is the usual form, the second is used before a vowel or a silent 'h'.
vieux   vieille   vieux   vieilles
vieil
beau   belle   beaux   belles
bel
nouveau   nouvelle   nouveaux   nouvelles
nouvel

Position of adjectives

Generally speaking, adjectives in French **follow** the noun.
EXAMPLE:
une jupe noire – a black skirt
des livres intéressants – some interesting books

However, a number of common adjectives precede the noun:
grand, petit, bon, mauvais, beau, joli, jeune, vieux, gros, premier, dernier, autre.
EXAMPLE:
une belle peinture – a beautiful painting
la dernière fois – the last time

Ce, cette, ces, etc.

These are sometimes known as **'demonstrative'** adjectives.
They may mean either **this** or **that**, **these** or **those**.
EXAMPLE:
ce garçon – this (that) boy
However, before a masculine noun beginning with a vowel or silent 'h':
cet homme – this (that) man
cette dame – this (that) lady
ces garçons et ces filles
these (those) boys and these (those) girls

If the meaning is not clear, you add —ci (this) or —là (that).
EXAMPLE:
Donne-moi ce livre-là s'il te plaît.
Give me that book, please.

143

Celui, celle, ceux, celles

These words, which are called '**demonstrative pronouns**', have already been mentioned in the GRAMMAR SUMMARY to Dossier 3, page 47, where they were shown used to answer questions lequel? laquelle? etc.
Here are some more uses of these words:

1 Tu connais ces hommes? Je connais celui au nez rouge.
  Do you know those men? I know the one with a red nose.
  Ces jupes ne sont pas mal, mais celles-là sont plus jolies.
  These skirts aren't bad, but those over there are prettier.

2 Celui-ci etc. may mean 'the latter'.
  Celui-là etc. may mean 'the former'.
  EXAMPLE:
  Marie et Chantal se connaissent depuis longtemps. Celle-ci est petite et blonde, mais celle-là est grande et brune.

Le mien, la mienne, etc.

These are known as '**possessive pronouns**'. Here is a complete list:

masculine singular	feminine singular	masculine plural	feminine plural	meaning
le mien	la mienne	les miens	les miennes	mine
le tien	la tienne	les tiens	les tiennes	yours
le sien	la sienne	les siens	les siennes	his/her
le nôtre	la nôtre	les nôtres	les nôtres	ours
le vôtre	la vôtre	les vôtres	les vôtres	yours
le leur	la leur	les leurs	les leurs	theirs

EXAMPLE:
Si tu n'as pas de stylo tu peux emprunter le mien.
If you haven't got a pen, you can borrow mine.

Mon, ma, mes, etc.

These are sometimes known as '**possessive adjectives**'. The forms are as follows:

masculine singular	feminine singular	plural (*m* and *f*)
mon	ma	mes
ton	ta	tes
son	sa	ses
notre	notre	nos
votre	votre	vos
leur	leur	leurs

● NOTE
These obey the same rule as other adjectives, i.e. they agree with the noun they describe, therefore, 'sa mère' may mean 'his mother' or 'her mother', according to context. It must be 'sa' since 'mère' is feminine.

It is possible to express ownership in the following ways:
A qui est ce stylo? – Whose pen is this?
C'est mon stylo – It's my pen.
or
C'est à moi. – It's mine.

Du, de la, des, etc.

For the use of these words, see the GRAMMAR SUMMARY to Dossier 4, page 60.
● Note that 'de' may be used on its own to mean '**from**'.
  EXAMPLE:
  Il est de Marseille. – He is from Marseille.
Note the following expressions:
jouer du piano – to play the piano
jouer de la guitare – to play the guitar

Au, a la, aux, etc.

These words mean **'to'** or **'at'** the.

masculine singular	**feminine singular**	**plural** (*m* and *f*)
au parc	à la piscine	aux magasins
before vowel or silent 'h'	**before vowel or silent 'h'**	
à l'hôtel	à l'épicerie	

- Note the following expressions:
  jouer au football – to play football
  jouer au tennis – to play tennis
  jouer à la pétanque – to play bowls
  jouer aux cartes – to play cards

Expressions with parts of the body

In general, the definite article is used with parts of the body much more often in French than in English.
Elle a les cheveux blonds. – She has fair hair.
Il a levé la tête. – He raised his head.
Elle s'est lavé les mains. – She washed her hands.
Il s'est coupé le doigt. – He cut his finger.
Il s'est fait mal au genou. – He hurt his knee.
J'ai mal à l'estomac. – I have stomach ache.
J'ai mal aux dents. – I have toothache.
J'ai mal à la gorge. – I have a sore throat.
J'ai mal au coeur. – I feel sick.
Le garçon aux grandes oreilles. – The boy with big ears.

Useful adjectives

It is not suggested that you will necessarily want to use all the adjectives below in your own oral and written work. However, they provide a useful basic list for translation and comprehension. Try to add others to the list as you come across them. In all cases, the masculine singular is given.

aimable – kind, friendly
cher – dear
bon marché – cheap
triste – sad
drôle – funny
heureux – happy
content – happy, pleased
bizarre – strange, odd
affreux – awful, frightful
épouvantable – frightful
courageux – brave
merveilleux – marvellous
féroce – fierce
sauvage – wild (not tame) **N.B.** un canard sauvage – a wild duck, **not** a savage duck!
mûr – ripe
court – short
fatigué – tired
lourd – heavy
léger – light
sale – dirty
propre – clean (une chambre propre – a clean room)
       own (ma propre chambre – my own room)
mince – slim
maigre – thin
clair – light, clear
sombre – dark
foncé – dark (of colours)
chaud – hot
froid – cold
tiède – warm
plein – full
vide – empty
prêt – ready
fort – strong
faible – weak
dur – hard
mou – soft
ennuyeux – boring
occupé – occupied, taken (a seat etc.)
libre – free, vacant
gratuit – free (of charge)
agréable – pleasant
sûr – sure
fier – proud
sec – dry
mouillé – wet
trempé – soaked
déçu – disappointed
trompé – deceived
doux – sweet
amer – bitter
nouveau – new
neuf – brand new (une robe neuve)

145

roux – red (only of hair, beard)
inconnu – unknown
étrange – strange
étroit – narrow
large – wide
épais – thick
chauve – bald
ravi – delighted
enchanté – delighted
haut – high
bas – low
rond – round
carré – square
trapu – sturdy, stocky
laid – ugly
vilain – ugly
étonné – surprised
profond – deep
debout – standing
spécial – unusual
tranquille – calm
rôti – roast
maladroit – clumsy
pareil – same (Les deux robes étaient pareilles.)
    (The two dresses were the same.)
pareil – such (Je n'ai jamais entendu une
    chose pareille.)
    (I never heard of such a thing.)
tel – such (Je n'ai jamais connu un tel enfant.)
    (I have never known such a child.)
sain – healthy
malsain – unhealthy
poussiéreux – dusty
graisseux – greasy

Adverbs

- The general rule for forming adverbs in French is to add **—ment** to the feminine form of the adjective.
  EXAMPLE:
  malheureux   malheureusement
  (unfortunate) (unfortunately)
  complet   complètement
  (complete)   (completely)

- If the masculine singular of the adjective already ends in a vowel, **—ment** is added to this.
  EXAMPLE:
  rapide (quick)   rapidement (quickly)
  vrai (real)   vraiment (really)

- Adjectives ending in **—ent** or **—ant** usually change this to **—emment** or **—amment** for the adverb.
  EXAMPLE:
  évident (evident)
     évidemment (evidently)
  bruyant (noisy)   bruyamment (noisily)

- A few adjectives add an acute accent to the 'e' when forming the adverb.
  EXAMPLE:
  profond (deep)   profondément (deeply)

- In a few expressions adjectives are used as adverbs (and are, therefore, invariable).
  EXAMPLE
  travailler dur – to work hard
  crier fort – to shout loudly

- Remember that the following are adverbs, not adjectives, therefore you **do not** need to add **—ment**:
  vite – quickly
  soudain – suddenly
  The following must be learn by heart:

Adjective	**Adverb**
bon – good	bien – well
meilleur – better	mieux – better
petit – little	peu – little
mauvais – bad	mal – badly

Position of adverbs

- The rule about this is stricter in French than in English.
  The adverb in French should always immediately follow the verb.
  EXAMPLE:
  Elle travaille bien.
  Il avançait lentement.

- In a compound tense, such as the perfect or pluperfect, the adverb should be placed between the auxiliary and the past participle.
  EXAMPLE:
  Il est vite sorti.
  J'avais complètement oublié.
  There are exceptions to this rule, but they are so rare that you do not need to bother about them at this stage.

The present participle

In English, the present participle is the part of the verb which ends in **—ing**, e.g. giving, doing, saying.
In French, it always ends in **—ant**, e.g. donnant, faisant, disant.
The main uses of the present participle in French are:

1. a **En + present participle** (by, on, when, while . . .)
   EXAMPLE:
   En arrivant à la gare, elle a acheté un billet.
   On arriving at the station, she bought a ticket.

   b **Tout en + present participle** (when two actions occur at the same time)
   EXAMPLE:
   Tout en parlant, elle a versé une tasse de café.
   As she was talking, she poured out a cup of coffee.

2. **As an adjective** (in this case it must agree with the noun like any other adjective)
   EXAMPLE:
   une dame souriante – a smiling lady
   des enfants charmants – some charming children

NOTES

1. When the **—ing** adjective does not refer to the subject of the sentence you cannot use a present participle in French, you must use **qui and a verb**.
   EXAMPLE:
   J'ai vu un homme qui portait un chapeau melon.
   I saw a man wearing a bowler hat.

2. Look at the example in **1a** above.
   Instead of:
   En arrivant à la gare, elle . . .
   you could also have:
   Arrivée à la gare, elle . . .
   or:
   Etant arrivée à la gare, elle . . .

Expressions of place and position

sur – on
sous – under
dans – in
devant – in front of
derrière – behind
à côté de – beside, next to
en face de – opposite
au coin – on the corner,
loin de – far from
près de – near to
● Note this construction:
   C'est loin? Non c'est à cent mètres.
partout – everywhere
nulle part – nowhere
ailleurs – elsewhere
en haut – up above
en bas – down below
à droite – to the right
à gauche – to the left
tout droit – straight on

Greetings, exclamations, etc.

Bonjour – Good morning, Good afternoon.
Bonsoir – Good evening, Good night.
Bonne nuit – Good night. (only when you are actually going to bed)
Salut – Hallo. (can also be used for goodbye)
A bientôt – See you soon. (i.e. at the weekend, next week)
Mon dieu! – Good heavens! (**not** Good God!)
Zut alors! – A mild exclamation of annoyance.
Va-t-en. – Go away.
Tais-toi. – Be quiet, shut up.
Dépêche-toi.
Dépêchez-vous. } — Hurry up.
Attention! – Look out!
Fais attention!
Faites attention! } — Be careful!
s'il te plaît
s'il vous plaît } — please
Au revoir. – Goodbye.

VOCABULARY UNDER TOPIC HEADINGS

The home

la maison – the house
l'appartement (m) – the flat
l'immeuble – the block of flats
le vestibule – the hall
la pièce – the room
la salle à manger – the dining room
la salle de séjour – the living room
le salon – the lounge
l'escalier – the stairs
le palier – the landing
la chambre (à coucher) – the bedroom
la salle de bains – the bath room
la cuisine – the kitchen
le grenier – the attic
le sous-sol – the basement
le toit – the roof
la cheminée – the chimney, fireplace
le mur – the wall
la grille – the gate
le plancher – the floor
le plafond – the ceiling

le lit – the bed
l'armoire (f) – the wardrobe
la coiffeuse – the dressing table
la commode – the chest of drawers
l'étagère (f) – the shelf, set of shelves
le lavabo – the washbasin
la baignoire – the bath
la table – the table
la chaise – the chair
le buffet – the sideboard
le fauteuil – the armchair
le canapé – the settee
le téléviseur
le poste de télévision } – the television set
le tourne-disques – the record-player
la radio – the radio
la lampe – the lamp
le tableau – the picture
l'évier – the sink
la cuisinière électrique – the electric cooker
la cuisinière à gaz – the gas cooker
le placard – the cupboard
le frigo – the fridge
le congélateur – the freezer
la machine à laver – the washing machine
l'aspirateur – the vacuum cleaner (Hoover)
le tapis – the carpet
la moquette – the (fitted) carpet
le rideau – the curtain

The family

le père – the father
la mère – the mother
le fils – the son
la fille – the daughter
le frère – the brother
la soeur – the sister
le grand-père – the grandfather
la grand-mère – the grandmother
l'oncle – the uncle
la tante – the aunt

le cousin, la cousine – the cousin
le mari – the husband
la femme – the wife
le beau-père – the father-in-law
la belle mère – the mother-in-law
le neveu – the nephew
la nièce – the niece
le petit-fils – the grandson
la petite-fille – the granddaughter

Meals, food and drink

le petit déjeuner – the breakfast
le déjeuner – the lunch
le dîner – the dinner
le souper – the supper
la nappe – the tablecloth
le couteau – the knife
la fourchette – the fork
la cuiller, cuillère – the spoon
l'assiette (f) – the plate
la soucoupe – the saucer
la tasse – the cup
le verre – the glass
le bol – the bowl
le plat – the dish
la théière – the teapot
la cafetière – the coffeepot
mettre le couvert – to lay the table
le pain – the bread
le beurre – the butter
la confiture – the jam
le sucre – the sugar
le thé – the tea
le café – the coffee
le lait – the milk
la viande – the meat
le boeuf – the beef
le veau – the veal
le porc – the pork
le gigot – the leg of lamb
les légumes – the vegetables
les petits pois – the peas
les haricots verts – the green beans
les carottes – the carrots
le chou-fleur – the cauliflower
le chou – the cabbage
la tomate – the tomato
les pommes de terre – the potatoes
les frites – the chips
le poulet – the chicken
le poisson – the fish
les oeufs – the eggs
la glace – the ice cream
la pomme – the apple
la poire – the pear
la banane – the banana
la fraise – the strawberry
la framboise – the raspberry
la pêche – the peach
le fromage – the cheese
le biscuit – the biscuit
la limonade – the lemonade
la bière – the beer
le vin – the wine
l'eau minérale – the mineral water

Clothes

la robe – dress
la jupe – skirt
le chemisier – shirt (woman's), blouse
le chandail – sweater, jumper
le tricot – jumper, cardigan
le manteau – coat (women's)
le chapeau – hat
l'écharpe – scarf (long)
le foulard – scarf (square)
les gants – gloves
le collant – tights
les bas – stockings
les chaussettes – socks
les chaussures – shoes
les pantoufles – slippers
la chemise de nuit – nightdress
le pyjama – pyjamas
la robe de chambre – dressing gown
le maillot de bain – swimming costume
le pantalon – trousers
le jean – jeans
la chemise – shirt (man's)
la veste – jacket
le pardessus – overcoat
l'imperméable (m) – raincoat
la cravate – tie
les bottes (f pl) – boots
le parapluie – umbrella
le sac (à main) – handbag
la serviette – briefcase
la montre – watch
le collier – necklace
les boucles d'oreilles – earrings
la bague – ring
l'alliance – wedding ring
le bracelet – bracelet

Shops and shopping

la boulangerie – the baker's shop
le boulanger – the baker
● Note:
  à la boulangerie } – at the baker's
  chez le boulanger
la boucherie – the butcher's shop
le boucher – the butcher
l'épicerie – the grocer's shop
l'épicier – the grocer
la confiserie – the sweet shop
la pâtisserie – the cake shop
la pharmacie – the chemist's shop
le pharmacien – the chemist
la quincaillerie – the hardware shop
la librairie – the bookshop
la papeterie – the stationery shop
l'alimentation – general food shop
libre-service – self-service
le supermarché – the supermarket
l'hypermarché – the hypermarket (very large supermarket)
le marché – the market
la charcuterie – the cold meat shop, delicatessen

le tabac – shop selling cigarettes, newspapers, sometimes stamps

la banque – the bank
la poste – the post office
un kilo – a kilo (weight)
une livre – a pound (weight and money)
un litre – a litre
un litre de lait – a litre of milk
une bouteille – a bottle
une boîte – a box, tin
une boîte d'allumettes – a box of matches
une boîte de sardines – a tin of sardines
un pot de confiture – a jar of jam
un paquet – a packet
un paquet de riz – a packet of rice
une tranche – a slice
une tranche de jambon – a slice of ham
le rayon – the department (in a large shop)
la caisse – the cash desk
le prix – the price
les soldes – the sales

Around the town

la mairie } – the town hall
l'hôtel de ville
la bibliothèque – the library
le cinéma – the cinema
le théâtre – the theatre
la piscine – the swimming pool
le commissariat – the police station
le syndicat d'initiative } – the tourist office
le bureau de tourisme
l'église – the church
la gare – the station
la gare routière – the bus station
la station de métro – the underground station
l'arrêt d'autobus – the bus stop
la rue – the street
une rue à sens unique – a one-way street
le carrefour – the crossroads
les feux – the traffic lights

la circulation – the traffic
les heures d'affluence } – the rush hour
les heures de pointe
le passage clouté – the zebra crossing
la rue piétonne – a pedestrians-only street
le camion – the lorry
la camionnette – the van
le poids lourd – heavy lorry, juggernaut
la voiture – the car
le chauffeur } – the driver
le conducteur
le chauffeur de taxi – the taxi driver
la moto – the motorbike
la bicyclette } – the bicycle
le vélo
le vélomoteur – the moped
le quartier – the district (of a town)
la banlieue – the suburbs

The body and health

le corps – the body	la jambe – the leg
le visage } – the face	le genou – the knee
la figure }	la cheville – the ankle
la tête – the head	le pied – the foot
les cheveux – the hair	l'orteil (m) } – the toe
l'oeil – the eye	le doigt de pied }
les yeux – the eyes	la dent – the tooth
le sourcil – the eyebrow	avoir mal à la tête – to have a headache
le cil – the eyelash	avoir mal à l'oreille – to have earache
le nez – the nose	avoir mal aux dents – to have toothache
la joue – the cheek	avoir mal à la gorge – to have a sore throat
la bouche – the mouth	avoir mal à l'estomac – to have stomach ache
le menton – the chin	avoir mal au coeur – to feel sick
le cou – the neck	avoir un rhume } –to have a cold
la gorge – the throat	être enrhumé }
l'épaule (f) – the shoulder	avoir la grippe – to have 'flu
la poitrine – the chest	se casser la jambe – to break one's leg
le dos – the back	se faire mal au genou – to hurt one's knee
la hanche – the hip	s'évanouir } – to faint,
l'estomac (m) – the stomach	perdre connaissance } – lose consciousness
le ventre – the belly	myope – short-sighted
le bras – the arm	aveugle – blind
le coude – the elbow	sourd – deaf
le poignet – the wrist	la piqûre – bite, sting (of insect)
la main – the hand	une blessure – a wound
le doigt – the finger	

Trades and professions

le médecin } – the doctor	l'avocat – the lawyer
le docteur }	l'auteur – the author
le prêtre – the priest	l'écrivain – the writer
le professeur – the teacher (secondary school)	le soldat – the soldier
l'instituteur (m) } – the teacher	le marin – the sailor
l'institutrice (f) } (primary school)	l'ouvrier – the workman
le boulanger – the baker	le mécanicien – the mechanic
le boucher – the butcher	le pharmacien – the chemist
l'épicier – the grocer	le coiffeur – the hairdresser
le marchand – the shopkeeper	l'employé – the clerk
le vendeur – the salesman	le fonctionnaire – the civil servant
la vendeuse – the saleswoman	la secrétaire – the secretary
l'infirmière – the nurse	l'ingénieur – the engineer
le juge – the judge	

Transport and travel

la gare – the station
le quai – the platform
le guichet – the ticket office
la consigne – the left-luggage office
l'horaire – the timetable
la banquette – the seat (in train, bus, etc.)
le filet – the luggage rack
le compartiment – the compartment
l'aéroport – the airport
l'avion – the 'plane
décoller – to take off
atterrir – to land
la salle d'attente – the waiting room
le voyageur – the traveller
le passager – the passenger
le bateau – the boat

le port – the port
la douane – the customs
le douanier – the customs official
l'autocar ⎫
le car ⎬ —the coach
une excursion en autocar – a coach trip
l'autoroute – the motorway (marked 'A' on maps)
la route nationale – the main road (marked 'N' on maps)
le chemin de fer – the railway
SNCF – French railways
la malle – the trunk
la valise – the suitcase
l'étiquette (f) – the label

In the country

le champ – the field
le bois – the wood
la forêt – the forest
la colline – the hill
la montagne – the mountain
la vallée – the valley
le fleuve – the river (large)
la rivière – the river
le ruisseau – the stream
la haie – the hedge
le fermier – the farmer
le taureau – the bull
la vache – the cow
le mouton – the sheep
le cochon – the pig
le cheval – the horse
la poule – the hen
le canard – the duck
la grange – the barn
la cour – the yard
le tracteur – the tractor
labourer – to plough

ADVICE ON EXAMINATIONS

The most important key to success in any examination is to have prepared for it by steady consistent work throughout the course. Assuming that you have done this, there are a number of additional ways in which you can help yourself achieve the best result of which you are capable. It is these ways which are dealt with here.

Revision

Begin this in good time – at least six weeks before the examination. Make a list of grammar points (tenses of verbs, direct object pronouns, construction with 'depuis' etc.) and decide how many you need to revise each week. Tick off the items on your list when you feel you know them. Remember that the points you revise first will need another quick revision at the end, so allow time for that.

Vocabulary is best revised under topic headings. Once again, make a list of topics (the titles of the dossiers in this book will give you a guide) and decide on one or two topics to cover each week. Choose a list of not more than twenty words to learn for a topic. Write them out – the lists in the REFERENCE SECTION will be useful for this. Remember to write down nouns with their gender. Never try to learn more than ten words at any one time. You may think you can learn more. You cannot, no one can. You will merely be wasting valuable time. If you wish to improve your vocabulary still further, this is best done by reading. Reread the texts in this book and in any other French book you may have. Ask at school if there are any readers you could borrow. This is far more valuable (and much less boring!) than learning lists of words.

Revise by writing things down. With every grammar point you revise write down an example with its translation in English. The next day write down the English sentence and see if you can put it into French. Then check and see if you have done it correctly. Do the same to test the vocabulary you have learnt. It may sound rather laborious, but writing things down is the only certain way to fix them in your mind, and until you have checked that you know one item there is no point in going on to the next. Make sure that you know all the really basic things such as numbers, dates, times, in French. Candidates lose marks every year through making elementary mistakes in French.

The examination

Reading and listening comprehension.

Make sure that you know whether you have to answer questions in English with a full sentence. Many CSE boards no longer require this, provided that your answer is intelligible. Read the questions carefully. Some examination boards put in brackets beside each question the number of marks allotted to the answer. This is useful, as it gives you an idea of the amount of detail expected. If this information is not given, look carefully at the wording of the question. 'State exactly...' or 'What precisely...?' usually mean that more than one item of information is required.
EXAMPLE:
If the sentence in a comprehension text is, 'Elle est partie à sept heures du matin.' a question on it might be, 'When exactly did she leave?' The answer required is, 'At seven o'clock in the morning.' Simply putting 'At seven o'clock' will only get you a half mark.

In Listening Comprehension, especially, whether it is on tape or read by your teacher, it is important to keep calm. Don't worry if you don't understand every word – you are not expected to do so. Relax, concentrate your mind on what you have to do, not on thinking how nervous you feel.

If your examination requires you to answer questions in French on a passage, remember that this is not really a comprehension test at all – it is a grammar test. You have to show that you know how to use pronouns, change direct to indirect speech, and so on. In other words it is a test of using and manipulating French.

Essay writing

Do remember that the purpose of this part of your examination is not to see if you can write a thrilling story, it is to see if you can write simple accurate French. Write short sentences using constructions which you know. Pay special attention to verbs. Remember that events in your narrative must be related in the perfect tense, and descriptions of people, scenes, weather, etc. must be in the imperfect.

Try to use other tenses if you can. Use a variety of constructions which you know, e.g. 'après avoir + past participle', 'décider de...', 'commencer à...', pronouns, etc. Link your sentences with phrases such as 'après une demi-heure' or 'un peu plus tard'. On the other hand, do not be tempted to include pre-learned material in your essay if it does not fit the subject. However good in itself such material may be, if it is irrelevant you will lose marks. Do make your essay the correct length. If it is too short or too long it will be penalised quite heavily.

Letter writing

Much that has been said about essay writing also applies to letter writing. It is most important to read the instructions for the letter very carefully in order to know what tense you must use. Let us take two typical examination letter questions.

1

'Write a letter to your French penfriend telling him/her what you usually do at the weekend.'
This letter needs to be written in the present tense.
EXAMPLE:
'Le samedi je joue au football, je fais des courses...'

2

'Write a letter to your French penfriend telling him/her what you did during the Christmas holidays.'
This letter needs to be written in the perfect tense.
EXAMPLE:
'Je suis allé..., j'ai visité..., etc.

In addition, learn **by heart** the correct beginnings and endings for formal and informal letters. Make sure that the layout of your letter is correct and that the date is accurately written in French.

The oral examination

For some examination boards the Oral is conducted by an external examiner, but more often it is conducted by your own teacher. In either case make sure you know exactly what form the examination takes, in what order you do the various parts of it – reading aloud, questions on a picture, rôle-play, etc. Your teacher will give you all this information in class. Listen carefully, make written notes on what he or she says, so that you know exactly what to expect. If your examination is one where you are given time to prepare something, e.g. a rôle-play, use that time purposefully. Think carefully what you are going to say, then say it over to yourself quietly several times.

Conclusion

Very few people really enjoy examinations, but if you have worked steadily and revised thoroughly, you should be able to go into your examination calmly and reasonably confidently.

In the examination room use your time wisely. Work out beforehand how much time you can spend on each question and stick to it. On a paper of three questions, say, an essay, a letter, and a translation, it is not much use writing a superb essay if you have no time to do the other two questions.

No one gets a hundred per cent in an examination so there is no need to panic if there are a few words you don't understand; the important point is to show what you do know as fully as possible.

Good luck!

Acknowledgements

The author and publisher are grateful to the following for the use of copyright material:
p. 106, Sempe/Goscinny, *Encore du Nicolas*, © Éditions Denoël; pp. 8 (Travail Oral 2), 58 (Travail Ecrit 1), 83, East Anglian Examinations Board; p. 95, Roger Vailland, *325 000 Francs*, © Éditions Buchet/Chastel; pp. 84, 118 (Listening Comprehensions), Institute of Linguists; p. 23 Jean-Claude Carrière, *Mon Oncle*, Éditions Robert Laffont; p. 44 (Travail Ecrit 3), C E Loveman, *Le Bon Chemin*, Thomas Nelson & Sons Ltd; p. 106 (Reading Comprehension 5), ouest france; Albertine Sarrazin, *L'Astragale*, © Société Nouvelle des Éditions Pauvert, 1965, 1979; pp. 130 (Travail Oral 2), 99 (Travail Ecrit 3) *Quelle Histoire*, A Wheaton & Co Ltd; p. 32 (Travail Ecrit 5), 68 (Listening Comprehension 2), 71 (Travail Ecrit 4), 82 (Reading Comprehension 4), 121 (Travail Ecrit 1), The London Regional Examinations Board; pp. 80 (Reading Comprehension 1 & 2), 94 (Reading Comprehension 2), 87 (Travail Oral 1), 120 (Travail Oral 3 & 4), 19 (Reading Comprehension 3), 117 (Reading Comprehension 4), 107 (Listening Comprehension 2) MIDI LIBRE; p. 126 (Reading Comprehension 3) from *Les six compagnons et l'homme des neiges*, Hachette International. Despite every effort, the publisher has been unsuccessful in seeking permission to use all of the copyright material which appears in this book. They ask the relevant copyright holders or their agents to contact them about this should the book succeed in coming into their hands.

They are particularly grateful to the following for the time and effort they have taken to provide the photographs included in this book; pp. 19, 96 (top), 115 (all) George Williams; pp. 1 (top & bottom left), 5, 17 (bottom left), 22, 37 (bottom right, top left), 42, 53, 55, 64, 85b, e, f, g, 103 (top right), 118, 129 Peter Hughes; pp. 1 (bottom right), 6, 17 (top left & right), 24 (both), 37 (top & bottom left), 39, 40 (both), 41 (both), 49 (all), 63 (all), 79 (top right & left, top & bottom right), 85 d, h; 86, 93 (all), 96 (bottom), 103 (bottom left & right, top left), 107, 125 (bottom left & right, top right), Keith Gibson; pp. 17 (bottom right), 31, 79 (top centre) J B Briggs; p. 23 Paul Webster; pp.2, 127 Thomson Holidays; pp. 81, 82, 87 French Government Tourist Office; p. 84 Townsend Thoresen; 85a Air France; 85c Biss Lancaster; p. 95 British Safety Council; p. 105 Nissan; p. 125 Topham Picture Library.
Cover: George Williams (top photo); Keith Gibson (bottom photos).

Finally they would like to thank Madeleine Bender for her help and valuable advice, Vincent Driver and Peter Frost for drawing the majority of illustrations and Francine Rouanet of the Alliance Française de Cambridge for helping prepare the cassette tape which accompanies this book.